OUR LADY OF GUADALUPE

Our Lady of Guadalupe

History and Meaning of the Apparitions

MANUELA TESTONI

Translated and Adapted by Jordan Aumann, O.P.

ALBA·HOUSE   NEW·YORK

SOCIETY OF ST. PAUL, 2187 VICTORY BLVD., STATEN ISLAND, NEW YORK 10314

ST PAULS

Originally published in Italian by Edizioni San Paolo, Milano, 1998, under the title *Le apparizioni della Madonna di Guadalupe: Storia e significato.*

Library of Congress Cataloging-in-Publication Data

Testoni, Manuela.
   [Apparizioni della Madonna di Guadalupe. English]
   Our Lady of Guadalupe : history and meaning of the apparitions / Manuela Testoni; translated and adapted by Jordan Aumann.
      p. cm.
   Includes bibliographical references.
   ISBN 0-8189-0897-1 (alk. paper)
   1. Guadalupe, Our Lady of.   I. Title.

  BT660.G8 T4913 2001
  232.91'7'097253—dc21

                                2001023952

Produced and designed in the United States of America by the Fathers and Brothers of the Society of St. Paul, 2187 Victory Boulevard, Staten Island, New York 10314-6603, as part of their communications apostolate.

ISBN: 0-8189-0897-1

Printing Information:

Current Printing - first digit   1   2   3   4   5   6   7   8   9   10

Year of Current Printing - first year shown

2001   2002   2003   2004   2005   2006   2007   2008   2009   2010

Table of Contents

Preface

I am happy to present to the public this interesting and well-docu-
mented book. It treats of the apparitions of Our Lady of Guadalupe
to Blessed Juan Diego. In this work the author examines the ancient sources pertaining to the Marian manifestations on the hill
called Tepeyac (near Mexico City) from December 9-12, 1531, and
also the historical testimony of the event from the beginning of
the 16th century to the present day. As a matter of fact, Guadalupe
can be studied in the context of faith or it can be examined in its
historical, social and cultural context. The author concentrates first
of all on the historical dimension, in order later to manifest the
theological and anthropological content of the Guadalupan message, where Mary and the prophetic figure of Juan Diego are placed
in relief, and to conclude finally in revealing the continuity of the
tradition of Guadalupe.

The approach to the events at Guadalupe is always fascinat-
ing and suggestive. What strikes me as very interesting in trying
to grasp the meaning of the apparitions of the Virgin of Guadalupe
is the encounter between the two worlds: the Aztec and the Spanish, the vision of the one and the other and the cultural tension
between these two peoples (chapter 1). The historical evaluation—
diligent, sober, and rigorously scientific—will open a new horizon
for many readers, a panoramic view of the distant past in its indigenous context, and it will serve as an introduction to the Aztec
society of those days, the witness of which gives us an indisput-
able cultural index to the rapport between humankind and divinity, myth and reality.

Some modern authors affirm that the events at Guadalupe are a mirror of the national conscience. In this book, after having analyzed the authentic documents, we can confirm that the origin, the history, the miraculous events and the consequences of the apparitions of the holy Virgin have been conserved in extraordinarily vivid detail from the 16th century right up until today: an historical record and a Marian veneration which time cannot erase. The indigenous spirit of the Mexicans is drawn to the Virgin of Guadalupe, resulting in an exaltation of the Mexican prehispanic past. At the same time there comes forth from the Virgin a power of identification: a loving mother who bestows total liberation, a focal point of unity for a world in tension, and the fulcrum of a patriotic renaissance. A fervent examination of the national spirit and the hope of finding a place in history following the decline of the "Fifth Sun" began with the *Morenita,* as she is affectionately called by devout Mexicans. By her maternal presence Mary tones down and softens the tensions between the military and the cultural, the religious and the social. A new people is born, which is modern day Mexico, but there also emerges a new family of God— the Church—which has one and the same faith, a praying community, marching along the way to the heavenly kingdom.

Scanning the pages of this book, after resolving the critical problem, one comes to the account of the apparitions as understood from a theocentric reading of the message of the Virgin (chapter 2). The fundamental value of Guadalupe becomes evident by scrutinizing the popular religiosity of the Mexican people, where symbol and myth, faith and culture, are intermingled, enabling us to discover the beauty and reality of Nahuatl theology manifested in the language of Mary and in the flowers miraculously blooming on the hillside and in the beautiful songs of the birds. Here we find neither legend nor poetry, dream nor fantasy; but rather the basic outline of an inculturated evangelization which also gives us a key to understanding the Puebla document (1979, nn. 282,446) and the Santo Domingo proposal (1992, n. 15).

Pope John Paul II conferred the title of Blessed on Juan Diego in May, 1990, and with the beatification, proclaimed him patron of the indigenous Mexicans and the poor. This historical figure and messenger of the Blessed Virgin had been neglected for too long. Besides bringing the reader up-to-date regarding studies, ancient and new, made about Juan Diego, here (in chapter 3) the biographical material that reveals the sanctity of Juan Diego is reviewed. As a result, the figure of the seer not only comes into focus but also, I would say with emphasis, the historical truth about him. Codex "1548" was discovered in a private collection in 1995 (the centenary of the crowning of the *tilma*), and a scientific study of it was published as an Appendix to the four volume *Enciclopedia Guadalupana* on March 30, 1997 confirming its importance. The Codex itself is considered to be the most ancient document pertaining to the apparitions at Guadalupe and it was dedicated to Juan Diego in the year of his death, 1548. It is signed by the Mexican historian, Antonio Valeriano (1520-1605), author of *Nican Mopohua*, and the renowned Spanish historian Bernardino de Sahagún, OFM (1500-1590), author of *La historia general de las cosas de le Nueva España*. This certainly provides a solid basis for the historical existence of Juan Diego and the truth of the apparitions.

The continuity of the Guadalupe tradition is studied from three points of view (chapter 4): those who favor the apparitions, those who reject the apparitions, and an intermediate group (to which the author of this book belongs). Even if, amidst the new material coming forth from further research, the Codex "1548" is scarcely mentioned, it is nevertheless discussed in this book with great attention to details in Appendix II. In fact, the presentation of Codex "1548", carefully prepared by a group of international experts, not only sheds new light on the Guadalupe event, but also destroys every "argument from silence" during the 16th century and the arguments of those who reject the apparitions.

Appendix I gathers together the precious early accounts of the apparitions, presenting at one and the same time a faithful translation and a smooth reading.

The summation of the conclusions is a stimulating and accurate commentary on the Puebla meeting, which we considered opportune to repeat: "As lived by our peoples, the Gospel draws them together in an historical and cultural reality that we call Latin America. This identity is luminously symbolized in the *mestizo* face of the Virgin of Guadalupe. Mary's was the maternal and compassionate face which she acquired from her proximity to Christ, with whom she invites us to enter into communion" (n. 28).

One of the most noteworthy and moving of the phenomena that followed upon the arrival of the Spaniards in Mexico—with its light and dark features—was the evangelization of Mexico by mendicant friars who were tireless missionaries and marvelous apostles who lived a holy life of poverty. But the real agent of the spiritual transformation of Mexico was Our Lady of Guadalupe. She is the star that illumined the pathway that led to the conversion of the indigenous people. She presented herself as the Mother of the redeemed and embraced them with her maternal love.

The present work is presented to the public at the dawning of the year 2000, the Jubilee Year of Redemption by Christ. Throughout the world there will be various kinds of celebrations, and at the Basilica of Guadalupe there will be an international gathering of priests and laity.

As we offer our congratulations and thanks to the author for this convincing and historically accurate account of the events at Guadalupe, we trust that it will be worthily received by its readers. I invite them not only to read these pages but also to be disposed to welcome other cultures in order to increase the knowledge among peoples in other continents. In this way the faith opens to new horizons, crosses frontiers, is strengthened through practice and gives a brilliant response to those who do not possess the faith. The reading of the book can thus become a form of contemplation and will provide an authentic encounter with the Mother of the Lord, who is the protagonist of the story, the teacher of the Gospel. Mary is always close to us, she always teaches us, and she accompanies us in our interior life, in our daily tasks, and produces the fruits of holiness (Puebla, n. 290). Our Lady of Guadalupe is the hope of our Latin American believers, hearers of the word, and servants of the kingdom. The presence of the Mexican people at the sanctuary of Guadalupe, besides manifesting the "power of the weak," which is the power of the Holy Spirit, is also the bond of a new humanity, where each one is perfectly identified. It is an encounter with a country that is free, and also an encounter with the People of God, gathered in prayer, where our tensions are eased, where we love one another and no one is ignored. It is a sacred space in which all share in the family and partake of the Eucharistic bread in poverty and joy. It is an exodus into a new land of promise, a point of arrival after a long journey and likewise a point of departure after having found hope in the Virgin who with her sweet and maternal gaze shows to all the light of a new day.

Valerio Maccagnan, OSM

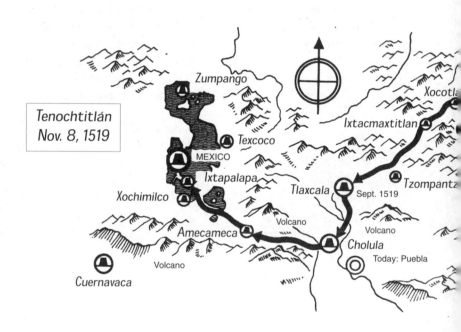

Tenochtitlán
Nov. 8, 1519

Zumpango

Xocotl

Ixtacmaxtitlan

Texcoco

MEXICO

Tzompantz

Ixtapalapa

Tlaxcala   Sept. 1519

Xochimilco

Volcano

Amecameca

Volcano

Cholula

Today: Puebla

Volcano

Cuernavaca

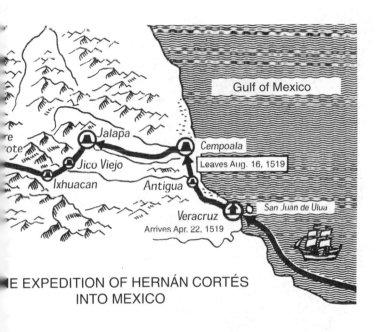

Gulf of Mexico

Jalapa

Jico Viejo

Ixhuacan

Antigua

Cempoala
Leaves Aug. 16, 1519

San Juan de Ulua

Veracruz
Arrives Apr. 22, 1519

IE EXPEDITION OF HERNÁN CORTÉS
INTO MEXICO

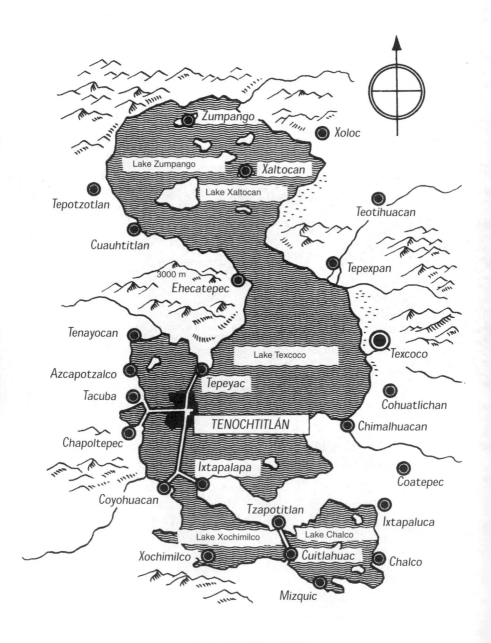

VALLEY OF MEXICO

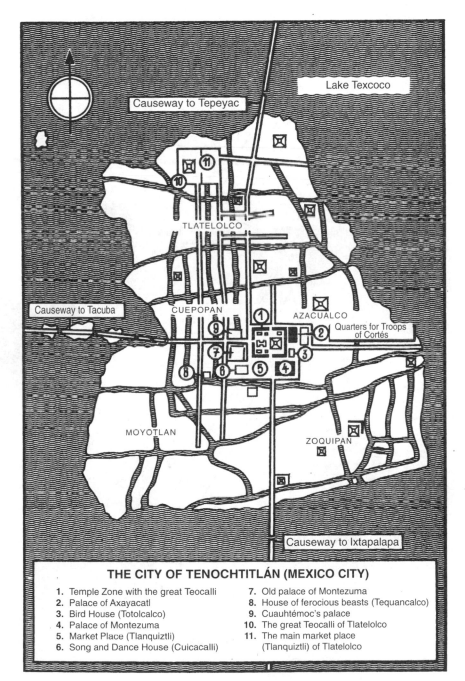

THE CITY OF TENOCHTITLÁN (MEXICO CITY)

1. Temple Zone with the great Teocalli
2. Palace of Axayacatl
3. Bird House (Totolcalco)
4. Palace of Montezuma
5. Market Place (Tlanquiztli)
6. Song and Dance House (Cuicacalli)
7. Old palace of Montezuma
8. House of ferocious beasts (Tequancalco)
9. Cuauhtémoc's palace
10. The great Teocalli of Tlatelolco
11. The main market place (Tlanquiztli) of Tlatelolco

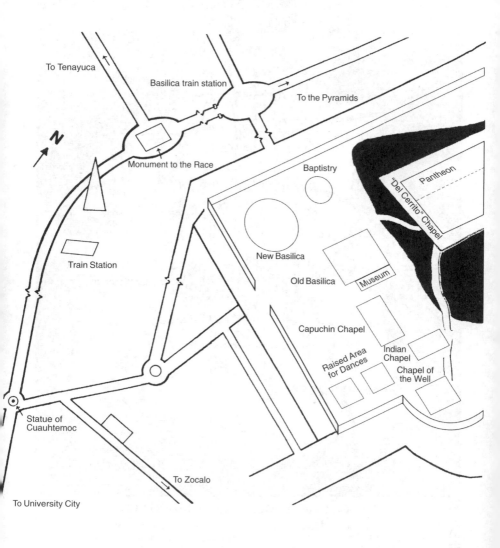

To Tenayuca

Basilica train station

To the Pyramids

N

Monument to the Race

Baptistry

Pantheon

"Del Cerrito" Chapel

New Basilica

Train Station

Old Basilica

Museum

Capuchin Chapel

Indian Chapel

Raised Area for Dances

Chapel of the Well

Statue of Cuauhtemoc

To Zocalo

To University City

Map of the "Villa Guadalupe"

Introduction

"The flowers appear on the earth,
the time of pruning the vines has come"
(Sg 2:12)

When, some years ago, I stood before the beautiful reproduction of Our Lady of Guadalupe which hangs above the main altar of the parish church of Santo Stefano d'Aveto in Genoa, Italy, I could not imagine that in a short time I would be at the feet of the original in the Basilica in Guadalupe, at the foot of Tepeyac Hill in Mexico City. Here, scarcely ten years after the arrival of the Spaniards and the fall of the Aztec Empire, God came very close to an oppressed people through the presence of his mother, who appeared to a native Indian named Juan Diego shortly after his conversion to Christianity. She frequently returned to Tepeyac as to her own home, and as a mother she never ceases to look after her children. In the intervening centuries, millions of Mexicans and Latin Americans have made the pilgrimage to Guadalupe, to relate to Our Lady as their own mother.

When the liturgical feast is celebrated on December 12, no one wants to miss it. For many people it is a time of personal pilgrimage; a time, as they say in Paraguay, "to return to their own valley." On December 11 the main streets of the city are filled with an unending procession of people from every state and condition of life: men, women and children, young people and old, from near and far, many of them traveling on foot for hours or even days. And one can see the residents of the city coming out of their houses to offer a cold drink, a cup of coffee, a piece of bread, with the warmth and spontaneity that one would use in greeting a long-awaited guest.

On December 12 the square in front of the Basilica is jammed with people who, with music and hymns and marvelous floral displays, will salute with reverence and joy the Madonna whom they acknowledge as their Queen. The offerings, too, will be generous because no one will present himself to his mother with empty hands. Soon the Basilica is filled with color and the aroma of sweet-smelling flowers. Some of the pilgrims are there in fulfillment of a vow or promise; some are crossing the square on their knees in penance; others are there in petition to Our Lady. Some groups of pilgrims break out in song while others improvise music and dancing that harks back to the devotion of the native people before the arrival of the Spaniards. At the same time the majority of the Mexicans and the pilgrims from other countries are reciting the rosary, which enables them to converse familiarly with Mary, with whom they have so much in common: poverty, simplicity, sacrifice, and hospitality.

Naturally, the liturgy of the Eucharist is the focal point of the celebration and it is there that the message of the apparitions is renewed and deepened. Although it is always very lively, the popular devotion constantly needs to be brought back to the essentials. The mother bestows abundant gifts on her children, but she also asks a sacrificial collaboration on the part of her children, namely, an authentic conversion.

The attention of all the pilgrims is fixed on the extraordinary and beautiful icon of Guadalupe, which remains intact in spite of the passage of centuries. It represents the *Morenita*, as she is affectionately called, a Lady of noble bearing, brown in color, with hands joined, dressed in rose-colored garb decorated with flower-designs. The sky-blue mantle, studded with golden stars, covers her head and descends to her feet, which rest on the crescent of the moon. At her back, the sun is resplendent in hundreds of rays of light.

We should not forget that the image of the Virgin is fundamental in the popular theology of Latin America. And it is not merely a question of a representation or image; Mary is felt to be actually present, so that her very person in some mysterious way exercises a protective function. Hence, Our Lady of Guadalupe is found everywhere: in the home, in offices, and even on street corners.

Of all the representations of the Blessed Virgin, we Europeans most frequently portray her under the title of the *Immaculata*, described in Genesis 3:15 ("I will put enmity between you and the woman, and between your offspring and hers; he will strike at your head, while you strike at his heel"), but the indigenous culture will also opt for other figures to transmit the same message. In fact, Guadalupe is a perfect example of an *inculturated evangelization*.

In order to understand how Tepeyac, dedicated by the Aztecs to the goddess Tonantzín, was transformed into a Marian sanctuary, it is interesting to read the account of the apparitions given in *Nican Mopohua*, a 16th-century manuscript composed by Antonio Valeriano, an Indian educated at the renowned Franciscan College of Santa Cruz in Tlatelolco (the present-day *Plaza de Tres Culturas*). On that spot which today is a verdant hill, but in 1531 was a barren and rugged landscape, the sweet singing of birds caught the attention of Juan Diego, who was on his way to Tlatelolco for the weekly catechism lesson offered by the Franciscan friars. When he looked in that direction, he saw a Lady in a halo of light, who graciously turned to him and asked him to tell the bishop her desire: to have a chapel dedicated to her on that very spot. Having failed in his first meeting with the bishop, Juan Diego thought of suggesting to her, whom he already recognized as the Mother of God, that she assign this task to someone of better standing and therefore more credible. But the choice of the Lady had fallen on him, so he must go a second time to the bishop who, being skeptical, asked for a sign. The Lady promised to provide one on the following day, but Juan Diego did not return the next day. On arriving back home, he had found that his uncle, with whom he lived, was suffering from a serious contagious disease.

At dawn on December 12 he decided to return to Tepeyac to find a priest, but he went by a different way lest he meet the Lady and be detained. Nevertheless, the Lady again appeared to him and she reassured him concerning his uncle, telling him to have confidence in her maternal care. She then directed him to go to the top of the hill, telling him that he would find there the sign requested by the bishop: sweet-smelling flowers that had miraculously sprouted in that arid soil populated with cactus and, what was even more, blooming in the middle of winter! Juan Diego was to show them only to the bishop. Later, when he unfolded his mantle to show the flowers to the bishop, the image of the Virgin whom today we venerate under the title of Guadalupe (a name which she herself had revealed to the old uncle when she later appeared to him and cured him) appeared on the *tilma* of Juan Diego. (According to Arabic etymology, the name means "river of light" or "river of love.")

The extraordinary event at Guadalupe is therefore an evangelizaton by means of words, symbols and miracles. The Nahuatl language is the simple language of faith; flowers and song encompass all the beauty, truth, grandeur, poetry, philosophy, and mystery of divinity. These were the means of communication with heaven. The arrival of the Spaniards was interpreted by the Aztecs as a catastrophe. It was understood as an abandonment by their own gods. Now, instead, the miraculous flowers and the song of the birds signified that communication with God was still open. The peasant, Juan Diego, was called through the song of the birds and the flowers that miraculously bloomed on the barren hill of Tepeyac to communicate with the Queen of heaven. From this sign and the presence of the Virgin sprang a message of hope, opening on new horizons, a new era, a new springtime of life. Culturally the indigenous world had disappeared, but the decline of the Aztec era of the "Fifth Sun" was in reality a new birth. The fusion of the two races would give birth to a new people and the dawning of what is Mexico today. With brilliant images and maternal tenderness the universal mother brought together conqueror and conquered into the one People of God.

Juan Diego was rewarded with the miracle of the imprint of the image of the Lady on his *tilma*, made of fabric woven from the fibers of the *maguey*, a typical Mexican *agave* plant. In the Nahuatl culture the *tilma* was not only an article of clothing; it also represented the identity and the personality of the person who wore it. Thus, Mary entered into the very life and heart of the Mexican people. It is an incontrovertible fact that Our Lady of Guadalupe is at the very center of Mexican popular religiosity. Guadalupe is a basic and dynamic element in the historical, social, religious and cultural development of the Mexican people.

At first the *tilma* was reserved in a little chapel constructed by order of the Franciscan bishop, Juan de Zumárraga, in the very place of the apparition. He entrusted its care to Juan Diego, who lived there for seventeen years until his death. The constant stream of the faithful led to the construction of the "Chapel of the Indians" in 1553 and later, in 1666, of the colonial church called *Cerrito*, over the spot on the "little hill" where the flowers had bloomed in abundance. Finally, in 1709, a much larger baroque style sanctuary having three naves, a dome and four external towers was constructed on the side of the hill. In recent years this ancient sanctuary has been closed to the public while being repaired and refurbished as a museum.

The chapel which contains the *tilma* today was inaugurated in 1976, and three years later Pope John Paul II greeted millions of the faithful from a balcony overlooking the façade where the words of the Madonna to Juan Diego are printed in letters of gold: "*¿No estoy yo aquí que soy tu Madre?*" ("Am I not here, who am your Mother?") From the same spot in 1990 he declared Juan Diego a Blessed.

Supported by 100 central pillars, with a capacity for 12,000 pilgrims, the basilica is shaped like an enormous tent which gathers the pilgrims under the mantle and loving gaze of Mary, who invites them to the Paschal mystery of her Son. The *tilma* is found at the center, above and behind the main altar which is made entirely of marble, at the sides of which there are two passageways which enable the pilgrims to pause beneath the "woman" of the Apocalypse, clothed in the sun and with the moon under her feet, the Mother of Mercy who intercedes for all believers. A series of electric lamps are suspended from the ceiling. The shrine opens at six in the morning with the first Mass of the day and on any day of the week one can observe crowds of people coming, even by foot, from the four corners of the city to greet the *Virgen Morena*. It is estimated that approximately 20,000 pilgrims visit the Basilica of Guadalupe every day.

The exaltation of Mary in Latin America is evident: in a *macho* atmosphere there is a tendency to idealize the mother, who holds a very special place in everyone's hearts. In celebrating her domestic virtues, the mother is awarded a power and an authority that is almost limitless. This cultural substratum is very conducive to devotion to the Virgin Mary, who is acclaimed in a typical Guadalupe expression, the "Mistress of Heaven" (*Señora del cielo*) on account of her nearness to God.

The question posed by Mary, "Am I not here, who am your Mother? Am I not the source of your joy? Are you not under the folds of my mantle, in the embrace of my arms?" These are the sentiments of a typical Mexican mother. The mother is always there where there is suffering and need, and she never abandons those who require her help. It is the mother who offers refuge under her mantle and is the symbol of authority in the home; it is to the mother's protective bosom that one turns in time of difficulty. Mary evangelizes as a mother, bringing the good news of the presence of God to those who suffer. She proclaims the good news of faith, love, pardon and peace; she promotes the unity between the two peoples and makes of them a new people. The *mestizo* face of the Lady of Guadalupe emerges at the beginning of the evangelization of Latin America, symbolizing the cultural and religious identity of this people, as stated in the Puebla document, n. 446. As a model for

the Church, Mary begins with great respect for the culture of the
people; she knows that the goal of evangelization is the transformation of the mentality of the people, but it must begin with the
anthropology of the people and the cultural symbolism proper to
those who are invited to give up their false conception of God and
their pagan religious practices.

Likewise, in the document issued by the Mexican Episcopal
Conference in 1978, *La presencia de Nuestra Señora de Guadalupe y
el compromiso evangelizador de nuestra fe*, Mary is proposed as a model
of the inculturation of the Gospel. In the document issued in Santo
Domingo (n. 299) we read that Mary is the Jewish woman who
represents the people of the Old Testament with all of their cultural reality and who is nevertheless open to the truth of the Gospel. She comes to the land of Mexico as the Mother of both the
natives and the Europeans who have merged with them, working
from the very beginning for a new cultural synthesis which is Latin
America, with a clear reference to the mariophany of Tepeyac.

But devotion to Our Lady of Guadalupe is in no way limited
to Latin America. Its fame has extended to the United States and
Canada as well. In the National Shrine of the Immaculate Conception in Washington, D.C., there is a chapel dedicated to Our
Lady of Guadalupe. And in Canada, since 1963, there is a sanctuary dedicated to Our Lady of Guadalupe in Johnstown, Nova
Scotia. In Japan, in the shrine of the martyrs of Nagasaki (1597),
among whom was the Mexican Franciscan Felipe de Jesús, there is
an altar dedicated to Our Lady of Guadalupe. Also in Europe there
are many places in which there is devotion to Our Lady, "the
Empress of the Americas": in France, England, Austria, Germany,
Switzerland, Finland, Ireland and Spain. At the sanctuary of Our
Lady of Czestochowa in Poland, Cardinal Wyszynski enthroned
Our Lady of Guadalupe.

In 1933, in the presence of Pope Pius XI and 226 Latin American bishops, a copy of the image of Our Lady of Guadalupe was
privileged to be solemnly placed in the *gloria* of Bernini in St. Peter's
Basilica. Also, near the tomb of St. Peter in the Vatican there is a

chapel dedicated to Our Lady of Guadalupe. But the oldest image of Our Lady of Guadalupe in Rome is found in the Augustinian church of Sant'Ildefonso. It was painted by Juan Correa in 1669 and brought to Rome in 1672. In 1932 a parish dedicated to Our Lady of Guadalupe was established in Monte Mario (Rome). Also on the *via Aurelia* in Rome there is a church dedicated to Our Lady of Guadalupe that is cared for by Mexican religious. In the convent of the Visitation one can admire a painting by the renowned Mexican artist, Miguel Cabrera, given to Pope Benedict XIV in 1752. When he saw it, the Pope exlaimed in the words of the Psalmist: "He has not done so with any other people."

The Virgin of Guadalupe is venerated in various parts of Italy, but the image mentioned at the beginning of this Introduction, in the church of Santo Stefano d'Aveto (Genoa), deserves special mention. The image was a gift from Cardinal Giuseppe Doria Pamphili, Secretary of State under Pope Pius VII and a descendent of the famous Doria family, navigators from Genoa. In the battle against the Turks at Lepanto in 1571, Admiral Giovanni Andrea Doria carried the image of Our Lady of Guadalupe on his ship. According to the annals of the Doria family, it was painted at the request of the Archbishop of Mexico City, Alonso de Montúfar, O.P. (1498-1573), as a gift for Philip II of Spain (1527-1598), who in turn gave it to Admiral Doria. As a result, the victory over the Turks at Lepanto was attributed to Our Lady of the Rosary and Our Lady of Guadalupe. It seems, therefore, that Italy possesses one of the most ancient copies of the image of Our Lady of Guadalupe, that is, from the 16th century.

When Charles III expelled the Jesuits from Spanish territories in 1767, numerous Mexican Jesuits found refuge in Italy, taking with them the devotion to Our Lady of Guadalupe. Among others, the motherhouse of the Ursuline nuns have an ancient image at their church in Arsoli (Lazio). In 1983 the Primate of Mexico arranged for a union between the sanctuary in Brescia and the sanctuary at Tepeyac. In the sanctuary at Albino, near Bergamo, there is a famous image of Our Lady of Guadalupe, given by the Jesuits of Puebla, Mexico, to the Italian tenor, Federico Gambarelli, who became well known in concert halls throughout Mexico. In the shrine at Loreto the sixth chapel is dedicated to Our Lady of Guadalupe, and in Bari in 1982 the first stone of the magnificent new church of Our Lady of Guadalupe was solemnly blessed.

The scope of this book is to review from an historical perspective the meaning of the Guadalupan event, in order to see the cultural and symbolic riches it contains as a patrimony for all people of all times. We shall begin with the historical aspect and then we shall move on to the theological and anthropological content of the apparitions allowing the profile of Juan Diego, who belonged to the ranks of the humble who rejoice in their intimate union with God and manifest it in their lives, to emerge. Finally, we shall discuss the continuity of the Guadalupe tradition from various points of view, taking into account any new developments.

The present work is meant to be a completely respectful approach to a culture that is markedly different from the one in which I was born, but one which I was called to accept and love, conscious of the fact that only that is evangelized which is loved.

I wish to express particular thanks to Fr. Valerio Maccagnan, O.S.M., an Italian Mariologist who has spent forty years in Latin America. He has honored me greatly by helping me find important keys to the literature on Guadalupe, supporting and assisting me out of his vast knowledge and experience.

OUR LADY OF GUADALUPE

CHAPTER ONE

The Historical Context

W E FEEL IT NECESSARY to present, however briefly and within certain limits, the salient characteristics of Aztec culture in order to clarify the religious and social elements in which Our Lady of Guadalupe manifested herself. An understanding of the historical context of the apparitions at Tepeyac is indispensable in view of the theme that we want to discuss, namely the meaning, and not only the history, of the message of Guadalupe.

The Aztec Empire: origins and social structure

The tribes of native Mexicans (Mexica) appeared in the Valley of Mexico in the middle of the 13th century, before the arrival of the Spaniards. A succession of cultures followed thereupon in a cadenced rhythm like the ebb and flow of the ocean. One savage tribe would merge with and replace the previous one that had become civilized and, becoming civilized itself, would fall victim to the next invasion. The history of the Mexica passed down by tradition indicates that, starting in 1168, one tribe came down from the north of Mexico, and in the course of a century and a half settled at the center of the country, in the muddy land around the great Lake Texcoco, which at that time occupied a great part of the Valley of Mexico. The Aztecs thus came into contact with people having a higher degree of civilization, such as the Toltecs

1

of Tula and those of the lake-dwelling cities who spoke Nahuatl, as did the Toltecs, but who did not have the same high degree of culture. Nevertheless, they had a belief that served as a basis of unity, namely, the conviction that they were "the people of the Sun." By the end of the 15th century they were known as the inhabitants of Anáhuac, the name given to the area around the shores of Lake Texcoco and eventually, by extension, to the entire country.

During their long migration up to this time, the Aztecs considered themselves to have been guided by a god they called Huitzilopochtli, a great sun god and warrior who spoke through the mouths of his priests. On command from the priests, and only in the place in which the sun, represented by the eagle, would land on the *nopal*—whose red fruit resembled the human heart—would the tribe finally be able to rest and found their city, Tenochtitlán. The fulfillment of the legend would signify that the people of the sun, chosen by Huitzilopochtli, had arrived in a place in which they would be able to spread out and become the instruments of their god. To this day the eagle in the act of devouring the serpent (reptiles infested the land up north in which the Mexica had lived for many years) is the national emblem of Mexico. Tenochtitlán, the capital of the Aztecs, was thus founded in 1325. A century later, having assimilated the culture of the Toltecs but remaining independent, the Aztecs entered upon the imperialist phase of their history.

From 1428 to 1440 they were governed by King Itzcoátl who, together with the king of Texcoco, had conquered the ancient rulers of Azcapotzalco and had established a triple alliance between Tenochtitlán, Texcoco and Tacuba. All other lesser and weaker tribes were compelled to be subservient and to pay exorbitant taxes to them. When the Spaniards arrived in 1519, the Aztec Empire extended from the Gulf of Mexico to the Pacific Ocean and south to Guatemala.

The social structure of the tribes at the time of the migration was very simple. The head of every family took part with the others in all discussions on important matters. The living standard was the same for all, namely, equality and poverty. Only the priests of Huitzilopochtli, the sun god and warrior, could be called a ruling class and they held the nucleus of power during that period. There were four distinct social classes: *tecuhtli*, the nobles, who were the ruling class; *macehuales*, the middle class, who had the right to vote (Juan Diego belonged to this group); *tlamaitl*, the working class, to which most soldiers belonged; *tlacotle* or slaves, persons convicted of crime and prisoners of war. These latter were generally chosen as the victims for human sacrifices.

By the beginning of the 16th century a significant change had taken place. Aztec society became differentiated, more complex and hierarchical; various functions were performed by various categories of persons. The change was profound and it took place in a relatively short time. The tribal democracy gave way to an aristocratic and imperial monarchy. The head of government or sovereign bore the title *tlatoani* (he who speaks). In the beginning, his power came from his right to speak in the Council of the Elders. Elected by high-ranking functionaries, he was the supreme head of the army. His primary duties related to the gods, and then to the people, for whom he was father and mother. Together with the sovereign, the other dignitaries governed as a group in the *Tlatocán* or supreme council of the city, which made decisions concerning foreign affairs. These dignitaries (*tecuhtli*) gave orders and shared power. The head of a village, city or province was always a person of standing, distinguished by his clothing and jewelry. He was supported by the citizens and even granted property. He was a police officer, a tax collector and a civil-service deputy. He was responsible for the smooth functioning of all the affairs entrusted to him. He was elected by his fellow citizens and remained in office as long as the sovereign willed.

The priests, who were regarded with great respect and reverence, were distinct from the military and civil authority, and they had a hierarchy parallel to that of the ruling class. The two high priests of Huitzilopochtli and of Tláloc held the title "Plumed Serpent," thus claiming the mark of divinity according to the myth of Quetzalcoátl and presenting themselves as his successors. There was a large class of priests, both male and female, who were experts in matters of worship and the functions connected with it. They exercised enormous power in Aztec society, both as interpreters of divinity as well as representatives of the greatest culture of the time. Among the duties of the priests the observance of the movements of the sun, moon, stars and planets was of special importance both for their scientific-religious implications and their practical application. The calendar, with its multiple series of combinations, was a religious matter as were the numerous predictions regarding the future, and for this reason it was necessary to know pictographic writing.

In a country that was constantly at war, military life offered to the valiant and ambitious a brilliant career. Of the four ranks in the military, the two highest were those of Eagle and Tiger. Any soldier who succeeded in capturing four prisoners was immediately admitted to the highest rank on the social scale.

A large number of Aztecs were also engaged in commercial ventures. Those who were members of the organizations that had a monopoly on trade with other nations were called *pochteca*. Those who dedicated themselves to commercial ventures could see their influence and power increase rapidly. Persons engaged in the arts were also numerous, and especially those who worked with plumes and jewelry. Those called *macehuales* were ordinary workers who tilled the soil and performed heavy collective tasks; they were drafted into military service and paid taxes. They were compensated by the distribution of goods, and their state in life, though lowly, was dignified. We find another category of persons between the free citizens and the class of slaves, namely, the *tlamaitl*, those who live with their family on the land that was parceled out to them. The farmer did not have the rights of citizenship but depended on the *padrón*, without being left completely under the control of a private power.

Last of all, there was the slave (*tlacotl*) who was the property of the state. He was treated benevolently, could possess goods and was allowed to marry a free woman. His situation was not permanent. These slaves were either prisoners of war who were not sacrificed immediately to the gods, or individuals who had committed crimes. Morality was strictly enforced, so that theft was punished with slavery; adultery, with stoning; murder, drunkenness and fraud with the death penalty. The legal system functioned daily and no allowance was made for appeals. Corrupt judges were condemned to death.

The majority of the population of Tenochtitlán was educated in the public schools (*telpochcalli*) which were designed to prepare the students for war. There were also schools of higher education, such as the *calmecác*, where the students followed a rigid discipline of self-control, self-denial and dedication to public service. The education imparted in the *calmecác* concentrated on the intellectual formation of the student, and these were the centers in which the *tlamatinime* or wise men imparted knowledge of the highest levels of Nahuatl culture. They tried to perfect the character of their students in two fundamental areas: the acquisition of wisdom through the proper use of reason, and strength of heart, through formation of the intellect and will. Two basic principles were at the basis of Nahuatl education: self-control through a series of privations to which the student had to become habituated, and knowledge of self and one's social role, imparted by one's father through repeated exhortations. Therefore, one should not be surprised that the children of the king, the upper classes and the wealthy would normally go to the *calmecác*. There was no class distinction of any kind in the educational system. As a matter of fact, the majority of the population were educated at the *telpochcalli*, where they would be transformed into warriors, but all the young men could go to one or another type of school. Women, however, were excluded from the *calmecác* unless they were of the nobility. Therefore it is certain that a warrior, who had received a distinctive type of formation, could attain to the highest kind of career. The high priests, however, were selected without any consideration of their origin; they could be sons of ordinary citizens. Moreover, an ordinary citizen could be invested as emperor and that would make him a member of the ruling class. The Aztec society was open, fluid and interactive.

The Aztec vision of the world

The Aztecs pictured the world in the shape of a Maltese cross. The east, represented by the extension at the top was a region of light and fertility; the north, the extension on the left, was an area of darkness and aridity; the west, the bottom arm, was a region of clouds and the origin of man; and the south, the area at the right, was that of the noonday sun and the god Huitzilopochtli. The Aztecs had a very detailed knowledge of astronomy and two kinds of calendar. The solar year of 365 days was divided into 18 months of 20 days each, with 5 days extra called *nemonteni*, and during this time there could occur some extraordinary event, either beneficial or harmful. The entire cycle lasted 52 years, but there was another longer period in Mexican chronology that lasted twice that long, or 104 years. Each 52 year period always began with "1 Acátl", the year of the east, the first day of the "Fifth Sun"; this indicates that the era in which the Aztecs lived was dominated by the east and by Quetzalcoátl, who sacrificed himself only to reappear again in the east.

Parallel to the solar calendar was the ritual or astrological calendar of 260 days, divided into 20 series of 13 days. Each series was dedicated to a god and was thought to be either beneficial or harmful depending on the significance of the first day.

All Aztec cosmology was dominated by the image of the four points of the compass, to which a fifth was added, namely, the center, represented by the sun. This concept is found in all the religious portrayals of popular Aztec devotion. The most familiar Nahuatl pictograph is a figure that, while having infinite variations, was always composed of four points united around a center (the sun: Huitzilopochtli), an arrangement called a quincunx. The number five represented the center, which constituted the point of contact between heaven and earth. Thus, what is known as the *flor azteca* or Aztec flower (present on the mantle of Our Lady of Guadalupe) has four yellow petals with a red circle in the center, symbolizing the meeting of heaven with earth.

Religion occupied a prominent position in the life of the Aztecs, and it would be difficult to find a pagan nation that was more devoted to its gods. They lived a life of severe abnegation and to their original lifestyle of nomadic hunters they added the customs of the agricultural people who had preceded them in the Valley of Mexico. Their religion was very open, in the sense that the Aztec conquerors incorporated into their own culture the religion and gods of the people they conquered. The pantheon of the Aztecs illustrates the tendency of the Aztecs to syncretism. Their principal god, as we have stated, was Huitzilopochtli, symbolized by the noonday sun in all its brilliance. He was the god of the hunters and warriors who had come down from the north and he belonged to a group of gods who were considered important to the population of northern Mexico. The same was true for Tezcatlipoca, the god of the evening sky, the wizard who saw all things in the reflection of an obsidian mirror (a lustrous volcanic glass, usually black in color); he was the protector of young warriors.

After making contact with the civilizations of the Valley of Mexico and the Toltec tradition, the Aztecs adopted the cult and the agrarian divinity of the sedentary tribes and added their god Tláloc to their pantheon of gods. Tláloc controlled the clouds and had charge of the rainy seasons, so much desired by the farmers during the anxious weeks of drought. Sun and rain were seen as *the* two powerful forces that dominated the world, and they were so closely related in the Aztec culture that they led to a synthesis in which the warrior tribes were converted to a sedentary life.

Quetzalcóatl, the plumed serpent-god, was the mythological priest-king of Tula, the capital city. His principal symbol was the plume or *quetzal* (the serpent, *coátl*, represented matter while the *quetzal* represented the heavens and the rain); his priests bore his name and his divine attributes. Quetzalcoátl is said to have formed a new humanity for which he provided corn, the basic food of the Mexican population, and for that reason he was also considered the god of agriculture. He was the creator god *par excellence*; he governed the weather and its annual cycles, and for this reason he was important to the calendar, numeration, writing and astronomical observations, in other words to the sciences of the times. Finally he was also the master of vegetation and water as well as the god of the wind. He never accepted human sacrifice and for that reason could not be part of the Aztec pantheon, but was transformed into an astral divinity, the planet Venus.

For the ancient Aztecs all the planets were divinized, but the moon, the sun and the planet Venus were especially significant for them. They believed that nature and man are not condemned to death forever; there is a resurrection, symbolized by the rising sun in the morning. Venus, the morning and evening star, disappears with the rising of the sun, only to reappear again the following day, all of which symbolizes death and rebirth. The transformation of Quetzalcoátl into the god of the morning star is an example of the tendency of the Aztecs to place their gods in the planetary sphere. In fact, their religion was essentially planetary because the hunters and warriors who came down from the north imposed their gods on the sedentary, agricultural people and rearranged the gods of the latter. The Aztecs were aware that Quetzalcoátl would return and take back Anáhuac (the land of Mexico), and hence his present status was only temporary. The god was to return from the east in the year that bears his name: C-1 Acátl. Consequently, when in 1519—in the Aztec calendar C-1 Acátl—the Spaniards landed at Veracruz, Montezuma believed that it was the feared return of Quetzalcoátl to his lands.

The Aztec religion with its minutely detailed and obligatory ritual and abundant mythology had a great influence on the daily life of the people. It imposed a rule of life but it also and especially gave an interpretation to the meaning of the world. In Aztec thought the supreme being, Ométeotl, was both male and female. In the generative act of Ométeotl, beyond space and time, one finds the origin and basis of everything that is and lives. Ométeotl is the only being totally rooted in self, and the Nahuatl world accepts as true only that which is rooted in something that is stable and permanent. The other key category of the vision of the world of the Aztecs is that of cycles. The earth, founded on Ométeotl, is not static but subject to the influence of cosmic forces in tension with each other. The idea of struggle or tension as applied in an anthropomorphic sense to the cosmic forces is precisely the form used by the wise men to explain the evolution or the age of the universe in which various cycles follow one another (the Aztecs used the word "Suns"). At the time of the Spanish conquest they were in the "Fifth Sun." The universe of the Aztecs was therefore a fragile one, constantly threatened with disappearance, and men had a rather insignificant role in it. Their only duty was to wage war and to die for the gods and, for the conservation of the world, to offer human blood in sacrifice.

The predominant element in the Aztec ritual was, in fact, human sacrifice. Human blood was indispensable for the life of the world insofar as it was maintained in life by the sun-god Huitzilopochtli. The sun itself was born out of sacrifice and blood. It was said that one night the gods were gathered together in Teotihuacán, the city of the gods, and one of them, Nanahuatzin, was offered the opportunity to cast himself into an immense funeral pyre from which he emerged as a star. But he remained immovable and he needed blood in order to put himself in motion. Thereupon the other gods sacrificed themselves, and the sun, taking life from their death, began its course through the heavens.

Here begins the cosmic drama in which humanity finds itself linked to the gods, because if the sun is to follow its course, and darkness is not to envelop the world, it is necessary to nourish it each day with the "precious liquid" of human blood. Hence, human sacrifice was a sacred duty contracted with the gods and also a necessity for the good of mankind, whose primary function is to give nourishment to "our mother and father, the earth and the sun." Nothing is born or lives except through the blood of victims of sacrifice. As soon as a child was born its father would inform it of its duty: to provide the blood of its enemies as drink and their bodies to the earth as food for the gods. The victim of these sacrifices was usually stretched out on a convex stone at the foot of the altar of Huitzilopochtli and held down, hands and feet, by four priests. A fifth priest opened the chest with an obsidian knife and extracted the heart. Other forms of sacrifice were by decapitation, suffocation, cremation or drowning. This ceremony is most repugnant to us, and when the Spaniards first witnessed it, they were convinced that this religion was diabolical in origin and that the gods of the Aztecs were devils.

Nevertheless, human sacrifice among the Aztecs was not motivated by cruelty or hatred; rather, it was their response—the only one they could conceive of—to the instability of the world which was constantly threatened with extinction. To save humanity and the world, blood was necessary. The person sacrificed was not an enemy to be eliminated but a messenger sent to the gods and clothed in quasi-divine dignity. All the descriptions of the ceremony (for example, those given to Bernardino de Sahagún by twenty Aztec informants) give the impression that there was a somewhat mystical relationship between the victim and the executioner. Thus, when a man captured a prisoner, he would say: "Here is my beloved son," and the victim would respond: "Here is my beloved father." The prisoner was certain of his fate and had been prepared to accept it stoically since infancy. What is more, if he were offered his life, he would refuse. To escape from the sacrifice was an unforgivable dishonor.

These considerations help us to understand the meaning of war for the early inhabitants of Mexico. Gradually the domination of the Aztecs was extended; their victories created an ever more vast pacified zone. But where would one find victims enough to provide nourishment for the gods? It was necessary always to wage war. That is the reason for the strange institution the Spaniards called the *guerra florida,* the flower war, which seems to have had its origin in 1450 at the hands of Tlacáetl, an adviser to Montezuma I (1440-1469). By common agreement the kings of Tenochtitlán, Texcoco and Tlacopan and the elders of Tlaxcala, Huexotzinco and Cholula decided that, instead of a war in the strict sense, they would organize occasional skirmishes after which any prisoners taken would be sacrificed to the gods. The scope of these struggles was to replace war with the capture of prisoners. War was not only a political activity but primarily a rite, a "holy" enterprise.

Arrival of the Spaniards

What happened with the arrival of the Spaniards was not so much a military engagement—the Aztecs preferred to establish peaceful cohabitation—as it was a confrontation of cultural values. There was a clash of two distinct visions of the world as soon as the foreigners set foot on Mexican soil. The Spaniards were received as gods who had come forth from the sea, as the ancient tradition had promised. One could say that it was for that reason that the Aztecs had renounced waging war against them, thinking that they would be powerless against the divine will. And it was precisely this mistaken judgment that opened the way for the ensuing military invasion.

Twenty years after the discovery of America, Mexico was still an unknown territory. By this time, the Spaniards were settled on many Caribbean islands, including Cuba. Although it was only a step to the Yucatán from Cuba, the sea currents made it impractical for the fragile seagoing vessels of the time. Hernán Cortés (1485-1547) had disembarked at Santo Domingo in search of treasure in 1504, and shortly thereafter he was named secretary to Diego Velázquez, the governor of Cuba, who entrusted to him an expedition to the land of gold.

The expedition set sail from Havana on February 18, 1519, with 10 ships, 100 sailors, 508 soldiers, 16 horses, 32 cannons and other pieces of artillery of lesser caliber. In the company of Cortés was also Bernal Díaz del Castillo, who would act as chronicler of the event. On April 22, 1519, the company disembarked a few kilometers north of what is today the modern city of Veracruz on the coast of the Gulf of Mexico.

On the way, they stopped at the island of Cozumel, in front of the Yucatán Peninsula, and rescued Jerónimo de Aguilar who had been shipwrecked on that coast in 1511, and learned the Mayan language. Some time later, at the mouth of the Grijalva River, the expedition's first armed battle with the natives took place and when peace was made, twenty slaves were given in homage to the Spaniards. Among them was Malinche, a woman who spoke Nahuatl and Mayan and was therefore very useful to the Spaniards as an interpreter. She later became Cortés' mistress. Cortés would speak in Spanish to Jerónimo de Aguilar, who would then translate into Mayan for Malinche, who would then translate into Nahuatl. A Mercederian friar, Padre Bartolomé de Olmedo, also accompanied Cortés and he tried to moderate the missionary zeal of the conquistadors.

The Spaniards disembarked on Good Friday, and on the following Sunday they solemnly celebrated the feast of Easter in the presence of Teutle, the governor of the place together with other nobles who had come to pay their respects to the Spaniards. At the hour of Vespers the Spaniards prayed on their knees before a wooden cross that had been erected on the shore and Fray Bartolomé tried to explain to the natives the basic Christian teaching on the passion, death and resurrection of Christ for our salvation, emphasizing at the same time that their Mexican gods were nothing more than devils.

Hernán Cortés told the governor, Teutle, of his desire to meet Emperor Montezuma II and to give to the emperor a helmet which Teutle had said resembled one that had been left by their ancestors. Montezuma accepted the helmet as a sign of the imminent return of Quetzalcoátl, the lord of Anáhuac. The Aztecs believed that Quetzalcoátl was bearded and had a pale complexion. In fact, everything about the Spaniards seemed uncanny to the Aztecs: their armor, their guns, and their horses, as well as their ships. Cortés, though, instead of accepting gifts from Montezuma and withdrawing with them pleased at the homage and the gifts, kept insisting that he wanted to penetrate further into the interior (desirous of conquering new territory). Meanwhile, the natives wanted to verify the identity of the foreigners, so they decided to put the Spaniards to a test. Do the Spaniards eat human flesh and blood or do they eat the grains of the earth as does Quetzalcoátl? A sacrifice was to be performed before their very eyes, as we know from the report of Bernardino de Sahagún, but it was immediately halted by order of Cortés, who insisted that they were not gods but men.

After establishing Villa Rica de la Veracruz and burning the ships of the followers of Velázquez so that they could not return to Cuba, Cortés began his trip to the interior of Mexico on August 16, 1519. Early in September the Spaniards arrived at Tlaxcala, and the natives came forth to wage war. They were easily defeated, however, by the military superiority of the Spaniards, so they made peace. Informed that they were enemies of the Aztecs, Cortés allied himself with them, to their great joy.

The next stage of the conquest involved Cholula, a vassal city of the Aztecs. Here both the natives of Cempoala, who had previously offered themselves as allies of Cortés, and those of Tlaxcala were suspected of plotting against the Spaniards. Cortés severely punished those accused of treason—which the Indians hotly denied—and commanded a slaughter of the natives and a sacking of the city. At the end of October the Spaniards abandoned Cholula, which now belonged to Charles V, King of Spain and Holy Roman Emperor.

On November 8, 1519, the Spaniards entered Tenochtitlán. Bernal Díaz del Castillo enthusiastically described what they beheld; it was like a dream. The city, which was ever expanding thanks to the land reclaimed from the water by the expertise of hydraulic engineers, extended over a rectangular area containing

plazas, temples, and botanical and zoological gardens. A network
of aqueducts carried drinking water to the center of the city. The
number of inhabitants (some 250,000) far surpassed many of the
most populous cities of Europe. The streets were somewhat nar-
row and many of them had canals which permitted the transport
of goods from the lake: tribute from the provinces, gold and silver
jewelry, plumes, cocoa, the bark for the making of parchment,
slaves and victims for human sacrifice.

They encountered the Emperor Montezuma in the city. He
came forth with great solemnity together with his officials and,
bowing, distributed crowns of gold and flowers, giving a short
speech of welcome (actually the prayer of the conquered to the
conquering god) and telling the Spaniards to be at ease as if in their
own homes. Later, in a private meeting with Cortés, Montezuma
gave him more gifts and stated that he was ready to serve Cortés
in any way possible. He was convinced, of course, that he found
himself face to face with those gods of whom the ancestors had
spoken and that they had returned to take possession of their lands.
(It should be noted that almost immediately upon his arrival in
Mexico, the natives had placed around the neck of Cortés a very
costly collar attributed to Quetzalcóatl.) As he had done on the
occasion of their first meeting, Cortés once again made a brief statement on Christian teaching and announced the coming of the
missionaries. He also spoke against the practice of human sacrifice.

The Spaniards were living under great psychological pressure,
worried that they had been welcomed into the city only to be
massacred. In spite of the splendid gathering arranged by
Montezuma, they feared that the emperor could change his mind
and they were prepared to attack or defend themselves. Consequently, they carefully noted the layout of the city and the direction in which they would be able to join their allies. They wanted
to be sure to cut off any free movement on the part of Montezuma.
As a matter fact, the emperor was practically a hostage; he was a
prisoner of the Spaniards, though treated with the respect and
honor that was his due.

In the springtime of 1520 news arrived at Tenochtitlán concerning the arrival at Veracruz of 19 ships and 1400 soldiers equipped with horses and cannons. They had been sent by Diego Velázquez, governor of Cuba, with orders to the commanding officer, Pánfilo de Narváez, to take Cortés prisoner. In the face of the military force at Villa Rica de la Veracruz, Cortés had to leave Tenochtitlán in early May to confront the troops sent against him, assigning the command in Tenochtitlán to Pedro de Alvarado. As noted by Sahagún, among the Aztecs that month was called Tóxcal and the first day of the month was dedicated to Tezcatlipoca. The feast was of the same rank as Easter for Christians. Pedro de Alvarado, fearing that at the end of the sacrifices, during the dancing, the Aztecs would attack the Spaniards, resolved to attack them first. When the celebration was reaching its climax, the Spaniards desecrated the statues of the gods and killed all the people who were in the courtyard of the Major Temple. Not one was able to escape. The uprising of the natives did not occur, however, because Emperor Montezuma had stated that no state of war existed, and that held them in check.

When Cortés returned to Tenochtitlán in the middle of June 1520, after persuading the troops of Narváez to join him with the prospect of a life of luxury, the Aztecs were ready to attack. The war began with the firing of a cannon by the Spaniards and it lasted for four days. The death of Emperor Montezuma II occurred sometime during those days.

During the night between June 30 and July 1 in 1520 the Spaniards, more concerned with loading themselves up with gold than with preparing for a possible attack, decided to leave the capital city. Turning onto the main street that led most quickly back to solid ground, they were discovered, surrounded and attacked. In the indescribable confusion that followed, hundreds of Spaniards were killed. The rout of the Spaniards has come down in history as the *noche triste* (the "Night of Sorrow"). Cortés escaped with the survivors to Tlaxcala, where he was warmly received.

Meanwhile, in Tenochtitlán rejoicing over the victory was

short-lived; the Aztecs had to face something more dangerous than the Spaniards. An epidemic of smallpox began to decimate the population. It was so severe that among its victims was the new *tlatoani*, Cuitláhuac, successor to Montezuma II. In May 1521, the Spaniards returned from Texcoco and began to attack the residents of Tenochtitlán, who took refuge in Tlatelolco, and there the struggle was concentrated. Cortés had divided his forces in order to orchestrate a simultaneous attack by brigantines and from the three main causeways of Ixtapalapa, Tacuba and Tepeyac. Nevertheless, against every expectation, Tenochtitlán did not surrender after the first or second or third attack; in fact, the assaults continued for ninety-three long days in which the Aztecs demonstrated their extraordinary resistance and their expertise in combat. They won various battles, captured and sacrificed dozens of Spaniards and a legion of Indians who were allies of the Spaniards, and they blockaded the ships in the lagoon. Finally, though, they were forced to yield to an invincible enemy: hunger. Tenochtitlán did not produce anything. Once the foodstuffs were consumed and the aqueduct and canoes destroyed, the city was doomed to a slow end, accelerated by the impatience of the Spaniards, the vendetta of the Indian allies, and the stubborn pride of the native Mexicans, who were forced to live with the corpses because they could not bury them.

Bernardino de Sahagún relates a final attempt to save the city. Cuauhtémoc, who succeeded Cuitláhuac as *tlatoani*, decided to dress up a captain of the army in the insignia of King Almizotl thinking that it would make him invincible. The documents of the Mexicans record that the Spaniards trembled with fear when they saw him, but it was an ephemeral victory. Everything was useless, and according to the Spaniards and their Indian allies, Cuauhtémoc was taken prisoner when he tried to escape. He died in captivity three years later. In the city the citizens fled in panic in every direction while the Spaniards searched in vain for hidden treasure. Tenochtitlán gradually became a pile of ruins. By August 13, 1521, the entire Aztec culture was overthrown forever, notwithstanding the rivers of blood from human sacrifices poured forth to save it.

The "New Spain"

Even today in the *Plaza de Tres Culturas* in Mexico City there is a stone memorial which states that "the fall of Tlatelolco was neither a triumph nor a defeat; it was the painful birth of the *mestizo* people." The invasion by foreigners was traumatic for the Indians. One of the Mexican songs that have come down to us from 1528 states: "Weep, my friends, weep. The Mexican nation has now vanished. The water has turned to vinegar, and also the food." In the next line, the lament turns into despair: "Let us die; let us die, because now all our friends in heaven are dead." In their encounter with the conquistadors the Mexicans found themselves confronted by entirely different human values and distinct social customs. Their old world had crumbled and they soon realized that they were facing a new life, but one without hope.

The fall of Tenochtitlán shocked the entire Aztec world. Instead of withdrawing after having exacted a tribute, the Spaniards dedicated themselves body and soul to make of Mexico a "New Spain." The situation was described in a letter to Charles V in early 1555 by the early Franciscan missionary, Toribio de Benavente, noted for his extreme poverty and humility. He did not hesitate to compare the radical changes of Aztec life to the plagues of Egypt: the spread of diseases brought to Mexico by the Europeans, the wars of conquest, the deprivations following upon military battles, the oppression by overzealous administrators, the high rate of taxation, the forced labor of the workers in the gold mines, the cost of constructing Mexico City on the ruins of Tenochtitlán, the various forms of slavery, and violence among the newcomers from Spain.

The numerical disproportion between the Indians and the Spaniards and the fact that the wives of the conquistadors did not accompany their husbands resulted in the biological fusion of the two races called *mestizaje*. The name *mestizo* was applied by the Spaniards to the children born of Indian women and Spanish conquistadors. The children were neither Spanish nor Mexican, neither European nor Aztec, but a blend, a product of American soil. The encounter between these two distinct worlds, the Spanish and the Aztec, introduced a distinction and tension that are still evident in the world of Latin America.

Historical evaluation

We cannot understand the conquest of Mexico without reviewing the medieval "reconquest" (*Reconquista*) of Spain by the Spaniards who regained dominion over the Iberian Peninsula by defeating the Muslims (or Moors [*moros*] as the Spaniards called them). The Moors conquered Spain in the 8th century, and their last stronghold in Granada was only defeated in 1492, during the reign of Ferdinand and Isabella. The Spaniards were determined to reclaim their land and to make of it a Christian nation. We may also say that the conquest of "the Indies" originated with the defeat of the Moors and the discovery of America in 1492. The Spaniards had always fought against infidels. Indeed, the *Reconquista* led the Spaniards to extend their influence to Italy and (along with the Portuguese) to Africa, Asia and the Americas. This was the period in which the Spanish and the Portuguese became great colonizing powers and Christian evangelizers, imposing their own values and institutions in the course of their long struggle to rule over foreign lands.

It was precisely at this time that Columbus presented his plan to sail to Asia, as he thought, across the Atlantic. After eight hundred years of war against the Muslims, the Spaniards were free at last to focus their energies and powers on other objectives. When they considered the wealth of those far-off countries and the countless number of souls who had not yet heard of Christ, the Spaniards were ready to dedicate their energies to evangelization and colonization. As one historian has put it, "From discovery they moved on to conquest, and from conquest to colonization, and thus a new empire was created."

From the moment that Columbus returned from San Salvador, Pope Alexander VI, fully informed about the discovery of new lands, granted to the Catholic Kings, Ferdinand and Isabella, the right of conquest and the obligation to convert the natives. The Spanish Crown carried out the conquest by adhering to a series of general principles enunciated for the first time by Queen Isabella, who desired to establish a sovereignty on the other side of the ocean, to convert the natives to Christianity, and to gain economic advantages. Once the natives were converted to the Christian religion, they would become free vassals of Spain, with the rights of full citizenship.

The conquistadors and the colonists, on the other hand, were thinking primarily of enriching themselves on the labor of the natives and gaining social position and titles. They were practical men, determined to get what they could and to do so ruthlessly. They were not wealthy men at the start, but came from poor families, eager to have others under their control and dominion. They were driven by cupidity for riches, and this is what impressed the natives. This cupidity did not limit itself to gold and other precious objects, soon seen to be ephemeral, but also to the *repartimientos* or repartitioning or redistribution of the Indians, commerce and the opening of new mines.

Anyone who went to the Indies necessarily carried with him the values, customs and characteristics of the region from which he came. That was a determining factor in the cultural and social foundation of the New World. In the early period of conquest and colonization the majority of the immigrants came from Andalucia, Estremadura and Castile. Hence, the traditional Spanish values and customs from those areas in which the *Reconquista* was still a vital factor played a definitive role in the formation of Latin American culture.

As discovery led to the conquest, so conquest was followed

by colonization. The settlements of the natives in Mexico were the most logical sites for the foundation of cities for the immigrant Spaniards. Cortés vigorously promoted colonization and by 1531 the most important center was Mexico City (Tenochtitlán).

Pedro Borges maintains that the civilizing of the indigenous American tribes was indissolubly connected to their Christianization. This meant that the Indians had to abandon their barbarous customs and idolatry and adapt to a new political system. Those governing and colonizing collaborated in this enterprise, but evangelization was entirely in the hands of the missionaries. It was necessary to prepare the Indians intellectually and politically before they could be taught other religious concepts. The King and the Council of the Indies (founded in 1524) were primarily responsible for civilizing the natives. In virtue of their royal patronage, the Kings of Spain functioned as delegates of the Pope in dealing with the New World.

The Spanish sovereigns provided the means and laid down the conditions for the divulgation of the Christian message, thus exercising a role that would eventually be assigned to the Congregation for the Propagation of the Faith (established in 1622). The officials and administrators, acting under the power of the Spanish Crown, collaborated very closely in the evangelization of Mexico, not only by carrying out the King's orders and regulations, but also by their own personal initiative. Moreover, we should not forget that in spite of their personal limitations, sins and contradictions, the Spaniards who came to the New World generally had a Christian conscience.

Missionary methodology

After the fall of Tenochtitlán, Cortés strictly forbade the practice of human sacrifice and the continuance of pagan religious rites. This prohibition was ratified by Charles V in 1523. Cortés also asked the King to arrange for more missionaries for Mexico, especially from the mendicant orders. As a result, until 1572 the Franciscans, Dominicans and Augustinians were in the front lines for the evangelization of New Spain and clearly outnumbered the diocesan clergy in the exercise of the apostolic ministry and missionary tasks. Three Franciscans embarked for New Spain in 1523, but the systematic missionary work would only begin with the arrival of a group of Franciscans known as the "twelve apostles" on May 13 of 1524. These were all well-educated men of proven virtue.

The great hope of these early Franciscans was that from their work of evangelization would be born a large community of Indian Christians who, under the paternal rather than authoritarian guidance of the missionaries, would model their community on that of the early Church. The Church in America, gifted with a high level of spirituality and a doctrine that was firmly based, would evangelize by means of Christian education, providing the whole gamut of educational institutions desired by the Holy See. Already in 1535 the Franciscans had founded the College of Santa Cruz of Tlatelolco for Indians of the upper class, where courses were taught, with excellent results, in three languages: Spanish, Latin and Nahuatl. The evangelization, though—at least in its early stages, consisted mainly in uprooting the indigenous culture and its cults by destroying all their religious symbols which were considered diabolical.

Precisely to combat idolatry, a considerable amount of ethnographic material was published. We recall in particular the frequently cited monumental work by Bernardino de Sahagún, *Historia general de las cosas de la Nueva España*. He had arrived in Mexico five years after the "twelve apostles" and became an outstanding linguist who taught at the College of Santa Cruz of Tlateloco. There were also translations of catechisms into the native languages, formularies for confession and Christian living, as well as grammars and dictionaries in the native tongues. This was all part of the missionary method used in the second half of the 16th century. Of particular interest is the work of Alfonso Molina, who had the task of translating the tenets of the Christian religion into Nahuatl for the benefit of his confreres as well as for the Indians. Can one, therefore, speak of the "inculturation" of the catechism, since catechisms were almost always translations of works originally published in Europe? Massimo Marcocchi is of the opinion that there was never any attempt to create a "Mexican" Church, because the Gospel message was proclaimed in the categories of European theology, without any adaptation. There was, rather, a spiritual conquest, for the missionaries set to work to organize splendid celebrations, processions and feasts with the greatest possible solemnity to offset the influence of the Aztec rites and promote a popular native Christianity. Use was also made of sacred dramas and morality plays in the native tongue in order to evangelize, instruct and edify the people. The liturgy, however, though carried out with a solemnity that appealed to the Indians, remained in Latin and the people basically remained spectators, unable to relate to it in depth.

The proof that in the first forty years the evangelizers were unable to dialogue on an equal footing and with respect for the Aztec culture is found in the *Libro de los Coloquios*, a book of discussions which the "twelve apostles" had with the wise men (the *tlamatinime*) of the area. It was a primitive attempt at evangelization. The report of these discussions, which is especially important for understanding pre-colonial thought, came into the hands of Bernardino de Sahagún in 1564 and were put in order by him. Actually, the *Libro de los Coloquios* should have been published together with the other works by Sahagún: *Doctrina Christiana* and *Psalmodía Christiana*, as is evident from the ecclesiastical approval printed on the frontispiece of the latter book. But only *Psalmodía Christiana* was printed, in 1583, and there is no news about the *Libro de los Coloquios* until 1922, when the Franciscan, Pascual Saura, accidentally found it in the Vatican Secret Archives. His confrere, Father Pou y Martí, published it in 1924.

The doctrine contained in the *Libro de los Coloquios* is the common teaching of the Church prior to the Council of Trent. It emphasizes the fundamental revealed text of Sacred Scripture more

than tradition. The exposition, which also corresponds with the
early missionary teaching, starts with the affirmation of the existence of one God, whose attributes are manifested on Mount Sinai.
Then, after asserting that Jesus, the just and merciful judge, is the
founder of the Church from which the missionaries were sent, it
compares the idols of the native pagans with devils.

We can understand very well the attitude of the first
Franciscan missionaries. The idols of the Aztecs had the appearance of monsters. Little by little the missionaries convinced the
natives that they had been deceived by these diabolical false gods,
even going so far as to declare that they had been conquered by
the Spaniards because the one true God had assisted in the conquest. God was therefore seen to be a warrior and vindicator. The
natives were told that they were not culpable since they had been
deceived. The missionaries had been sent to open their eyes and
to unmask the lies of the devil, thus restoring their human dignity
by illuminating their minds with the truth. The Aztec leaders
(*tlamatinime*), knowing that they were the vanquished, still did not
hesitate to defend themselves courageously against any attacks that
they considered unjustified. Their reasoning, which they expressed
in their dialogue with the missionaries, stemmed from their own
organized knowledge of the divinity and they stated their belief in
accordance with the traditions handed down for generations. They
pointed to Ométeotl, the god of duality, as the one who originated
the world and governs it.

The Aztec religion was populated by many divinities, per-
sonifications of cosmic powers and phenomena. As we have seen,
there was never a time or place in which the divine was not present,
represented by gods who protected, directed, and influenced daily
life and activity. Beyond the individual divinities, a sacred presence,
a God existing in every place, vaguely pantheistic, an undetermined,
impersonal Being of whom the particular divinities were manifestations, can likewise be perceived. In fact, the poet king
Netzahualcóyotl of Texcoco who died in 1472, not many years before the coming of the Spaniards, had arrived at an intuition of one

invisible God. This idea, therefore, was already present in the culture of the Valley of Mexico, a concept adopted by the Aztecs and
formulated by their wise men. The Judaeo-Christian idea of a personal God, however, seems to be absent from the Aztec mentality.

The dramatic response of the *tlamatinime* reveals their state
of soul. There is nothing for them to do but die, since, as they say—
and as factual reality confirms—their gods are dead. How, they ask,
is it possible for them to abandon their ancient rule of life? The
missionaries were basing their arguments on the words of Scripture, while the Aztec wise men were calling on the tradition of their
ancestors. For the Aztecs, it was not simply a question of particular precepts or norms but of a way of life.

Rather than a formal conversation, one has the impression
of assisting at a cultural monologue on the part of the "twelve
apostles." Only in the tangible symbol of Our Lady of Guadalupe,
proclaimed by a converted Indian, were these two worlds, until now
unknown to each other and in a state of enmity as a result of the
defeat of the Indians and the disdain and exploitation of their conquerors, able to come together. The time will come when there
will be a de facto inculturation of Christianity into the culture of
the Aztec world.

CHAPTER TWO

Guadalupe

THE SOURCES SPEAK of the dramatic situation at the beginning of the evangelization of Latin America: the frustration of the Indians who felt abandoned by their gods on the one hand, and on the other, the inability of the missionaries coming from the Old World to transmit a truly Christian experience to them. The greater part of the population remained indifferent to the new religion; the number of baptized was much lower than had been anticipated.

Nevertheless in that very situation an unexpected event took place, one of those interventions of grace of which theology speaks that changed the course of history. A fresco in the ancient convent in Ozumba, Mexico, portrays the beginning of Christian history in that country. It depicts the arrival of the first twelve Franciscan missionaries in 1524; the three adolescent Indians who gave their lives for their religion; and the apparition of Our Lady of Guadalupe, with Juan Diego kneeling at her feet and crowned with a halo. Mary is precisely the link that would unite the two worlds represented there. But before giving an account of the Guadalupe event, it is necessary to analyze the Guadalupe tradition from a critical point of view.

The critical problem

The first difficulty that emerges in examining the Guadalupe event is the lack of any official testimony, either on the part of the visionary or on the part of the Bishop of Mexico, Juan de Zumárraga, concerning the apparition of the Virgin Mary or any message received from her. Nevertheless, there are numerous writings, in the language of the natives (Nahuatl) and Spanish, that attest to a written and spoken tradition.

The historical sources concerning the apparition of the Virgin Mary in the 16th century are numerous (about twenty) and of great importance. A good number of original documents have been lost, although authentic copies of some of them can be found in various libraries in America and in Europe; for example, in Mexico City and Seville. Especially praiseworthy is the work of the Center of Guadalupan Studies, founded in 1975 in Mexico City, and its publication of the *Monumenta Historica Guadalupanensia* (I, II, III); its promotion of meetings on a national level since 1976; and the publication of the official organ of the Center, the magazine *Historia*, founded in 1977. As a result of their work, critical editions of the basic Guadalupan documents have been published and documents from both Aztec and Spanish sources which make reference to a Marian apparition that had actually occurred at a particular time and in a specified place have been identified. The most ancient of these goes back to 1537, or at the latest to 1539, and it comes from the city of Colima, Mexico. In November, 1537, Bartolomé López of Colima added a codicil to his will assigning a certain sum of money for Masses to be celebrated for him in the "House of the Virgin of Guadalupe." The town of Colima was founded by colonists from Mexico City where the Virgin of Guadalupe was invoked above all as the patroness of travelers. We have to be careful, however, to distinguish between the apparition and the cult.

There is a well-founded tradition regarding the cult. The writers who are called "apparitionists" (who believe that the apparitions are historically true, as distinct from the "anti-apparitionists," who believe the contrary) have satisfactorily proven the existence of a cult that was already widespread in the 16th century, because the little shrine constructed on the spot of the apparition was a true Marian sanctuary. We can point to the payment of stipends, bequests in wills, references to pilgrimages, songs (for example, the *Cantar de Atabal*, pagan in origin but adapted prior to 1547 as a Christian hymn that describes a solemn procession in which the image of the Madonna was transferred from the bishop's house to the little hermitage specifically constructed for that purpose by the bishop [Zumárraga, d. 1548]), and official church documents. In fact, from the First Mexican Episcopal Council (1554-1555) to modern times, the bishops of Mexico have always approved the devotion to Our Lady of Guadalupe. The Fifth Mexican Council in 1896 declared that "the apparition should be accepted and respected as it was in ancient times because it is based on an uninterrupted tradition and irrefutable documentation." In 1978 the Mexican Episcopal Conference issued a pastoral letter entitled *La presencia de Nuestra Señora de Guadalupe y el compromiso evangelizador de nuestra fe*.

In 1556, the second archbishop of Mexico City, Alonso de Montúfar, preached a sermon in the cathedral in which he reaffirmed his approval of the cult to Mary practiced on the hill of Tepeyac. A few days later the Provincial of the Franciscans, Fray Francisco de Bustamante, replied that the image of the Virgin at Tepeyac was not of supernatural origin but had been painted by the Indian, Marcos Cipac, and therefore the cult at Tepeyac should be prohibited because it could easily lead the natives back into idolatry. Archbishop Montúfar immediately initiated an investigation in which those questioned (who had heard Bustamante's sermon) denied the truth of what he had said, pointing to the widespread diffusion of the cult of Tepeyac. The matter remained unresolved; however the preponderance of the evidence points to the fact that the chapel at Tepeyac was, even at that early date, an authentic Marian sanctuary.

As regards the apparition, the most important document, apart from the image itself of the Virgin Mary on Juan Diego's *tilma*, is undoubtedly the *Nican Mopohua*, written in Nahuatl by an educated noble Indian, Antonio Valeriano (1520?-1605). Proficient in three languages, Nahuatl, Spanish and Latin, he had been a student at the College of Santa Cruz in Tlatelolco and served as an informant on Aztec history to Fray Bernardino de Sahagún. Antonio Valeriano was considered by all to be a man of high moral character and above suspicion, not only by his fellow-countrymen but also by the Spanish civil and religious authorities. For forty years he was governor of the Indians in Mexico City. The document *Nican Mopohua* begins with those two words in Nahuatl, which mean "Herein it is told."

The original account of the apparition was probably written around the middle of the 16th century and according to the style of that period. Antonio Valeriano gave the document to Fernando de Alva Ixtlilxóchitl (1578?-1650?), who left it to his son, Juan de Alva, who passed it on to the Jesuit Carlos de Sigüenza y Góngora (1645-1700). When he died, the document was left to the Jesuit College of Saints Peter and Paul in Mexico City. With the expulsion of the Jesuits from all Spanish territories in 1767, the document was lost.

The loss of the original document does not diminish the authenticity of its contents, as verified by numerous experts. For example, F.J. Burrus speaks of three copies in the Ramírez Collection in the New York Public Library. The *Nican Mopohua* was first printed in 1649 in Nahuatl by Luis Lasso de la Vega in a five part work bearing the general title *Huey Tlamahuizoltica*. Part One began with the solemn invocation, "O great Queen of Heaven," and was a prologue written by Luis Lasso de la Vega. Part Two was the *Nican Mopohua* of Antonio Valeriano in which the image impressed on the *tilma* is described in detail. Part Three was a narration of the miracles obtained by the Virgin of Guadalupe and is the work of Fernando de Alva Ixtlilxóchitl. Part Four, written by Luis Lasso de la Vega, talked about other images of the Madonna, coming back at the end to that of Tepeyac which had such a decisive influence on the conversion of the Indians to the Catholic faith. During that same period a Spanish version by Miguel Sánchez was published following the Nahuatl text of Antonio Valeriano which, on account of its authority, stood out from other accounts that undoubtedly were in circulation at the time as attested to by a 16th century work entitled *Inin Huey Tlamahuizóltzin*. Neither Luis Lasso de la Vega nor Miguel Sánchez give the name of the author of *Nican Mopohua*. It sufficed for them that their accounts were based on an authentic oral and written tradition.

The first light on the matter comes from Luis Becerra Tanco, who in the declarations released by the investigation, *Informaciones de 1666*, of which we shall speak later, affirms that he had heard his uncle Gaspar de l'iaves say that the author of the story of Guadalupe was "Juan Valeriano," a student from the nobility at the College of Saint James at Tlatelolco. On the basis of this affirmation, apart from the error in the name, he concluded that Valeriano must have been the author of the text concerning the apparition, but he was unable to prove it.

In the second half of the 17th century the authenticity of the *Nican Mopohua* was verified, thanks to Carlos de Sigüenza y Góngora, one of the most respected authorities on Mexican culture at the time. He declared under solemn oath that Antonio Valeriano was the author of *Nican Mopohua* and that he himself (Sigüenza y Góngora) possessed the original written in Valeriano's own hand. This statement is rightly considered the cornerstone on which rests the credibility of the account of the apparition, although we must keep in mind that with the suppression of the Jesuits, many documents were lost or destroyed. Consequently, although up to the present time we do not know what happened to the original document by Valeriano, it suffices for authentication that the verification of the document comes from one of the greatest experts on Mexican antiquity, as was Sigüenza y Góngora.

Recently, at the Centro de Estudios Guadalupanos, there was discovered a codex bearing the title "1548" in which the signature and the pictograph of Antonio Valeriano and the signature of Bernardino de Sahagún were discerned. The name of the Virgin and the name Juan Diego both appear twice in the document. The landscape of Tepeyac can be clearly distinguished and there is a reference to the apparition and to the death of Juan Diego, which occurred in 1548.

Though we still await the definitive judgment of history, this discovery confirms Valeriano as the author of *Nican Mopohua*. Father Angel María Garibay has advanced the hypothesis that Valeriano was a member of a team of informants who collaborated with Sahagún in the composition of his *Historia general de las cosas de la Nueva España*. He bases his hypothesis on the identical nature of the linguistic style of the historical data of Sahagún and that of the *Nican Mopohua*, concluding that the *Nican Mopohua*, like the *Historia*, was the work of such a team. Actually, he concludes, though Sahagún's sources gave him the necessary data to complete his monumental research, the final draft was the work of an outstanding ethnologist. Though Garabay's hypothesis is not accepted by the majority of experts, Arthur O. Anderson, another authority in this field, notes that the style of the description of the apparition is similar to that of the *Codex Florentino*. This would seem to confirm Garabay's hypothesis in the sense that the Guadalupe account can be dated back to the 16th century and was composed at the very latest between 1550 and 1570, the period in which Valeriano and the other humanists collaborated with Sahagún.

The apparitions

There are various translations of the *Nican Mopohua* into Spanish. We are using the most recent one (1978) by Father Mario Rojas Sánchez, which differs greatly from those that preceded it. In fact, Sánchez interprets the words of the Virgin in a way that puts God at the center, in accordance with Christian theology. Previously, on the other hand, authors presented a version that put emphasis on the Guadalupan image itself. The first Spanish version was written by Luis Becerra Tanco, *La felicidad de México*, but his translation was not always literal. In 1926, Primo Feliciano

Velásquez Rodríguez, historian, scholar, lawyer and journalist, did a Spanish translation of *Huey Tlamahuizoltica* for the Mexican Academy of Our Lady of Guadalupe. His translation, too, was more literary than literal. In 1978 the magazine *Historica* published posthumously a worthwhile translation by Angel María Garibay. But the best Spanish translation is the more recent one (1978) by Father Mario Rojas Sánchez, a priest of the diocese of Huejutla in the State of Hidalgo. Having studied in Mexico and abroad, he exercised his ministry in various institutions, collaborating in a number of publications. His years spent among those who spoke the Nahuatl language were invaluable to him in the preparation of this translation.

The protagonist of this singular event of the apparition of the Virgin was the Indian, Juan Diego (1474-1548), a childless widower who, though originally from Cuauhtitlán, now lived with his elderly uncle, Juan Bernardino, at Tulpetlac. He seems to have belonged to the working class and his primary occupation was very probably farming. His Indian name was Cuauhtlatoatzin, meaning "the one who speaks like an eagle." It is thought that he was baptized by Fray Toribio de Benavente, also known as Motolinía.

At dawn on Saturday, December 9, 1531, Juan Diego was traversing the hill of Tepeyac, located on the northern periphery of México-Tenochtitlán. He was on his way to Tlatelolco for his customary catechism lesson. Suddenly a very sweet musical sound caught his attention. He perceived the presence of something supernatural and was transported to another dimension, to an Eden of which our ancestors had spoken. He directed his glance toward the west, to the top of the hill from where the music had come, but it stopped and was replaced by a voice that tenderly called him by name. Juan Diego walked in the direction of the voice without any fear, but rather, with interior joy. He saw before him a Lady who invited him to approach (*the first apparition*). Her garb was radiant with light, as was the stone on which her feet rested, while the foggy ground was resplendent with the colors of the rainbow. Falling to his knees, he saw the Lady turn toward him maternally and reveal that she is the ever Virgin Mary, Mother of the one true God. She requested that a shrine be erected there so that she can reveal her Son to all the people who live in that land. She then told him to go to the bishop, Fray Juan de Zumárraga (1476-1548), and tell him what he has seen and heard. Juan Diego obeyed immediately but his first visit to the bishop's residence ended in failure.

Juan Diego returned to the Lady (*second apparition*) to ask her to find another messenger, worthy of more respect. But it was all in vain. He must be the one to carry out the assignment, so he yielded docilely to the desire of the Virgin.

The following day, Sunday, September 10, after the catechism class, Juan Diego went again to the residence of the bishop, who listened to him attentively but also with increasing skepticism, asking many questions. At the end of the visit, the bishop asked for a sign of the Virgin's request. Once Juan Diego had departed, he sent two Franciscan friars to follow him, but they soon lost sight of him. The Virgin, meanwhile, appeared again to Juan Diego (*third apparition*) and promised that she would give him the requested sign on the following day.

But on Monday Juan Diego did not keep the appointment. When he arrived home on Sunday he found that his uncle was very sick. The doctor could do nothing more than verify the serious illness, so the patient asked for a priest. Consequently, at the break of dawn on Tuesday, December 12, Juan Diego left for Tlatelolco. In order not to be detained by the Lady, he intended to bypass the hill of Tepeyac. All the same, she met him on the way (*fourth apparition*). Juan Diego confessed his anxiety to the Lady, who asked him to have trust in her: "Am I not here, who am your Mother? Why are you worried? Are you not under my glance?" Then she announced that his uncle would not die but would recover. She then sent Juan Diego to the top of the hill to gather some flowers that he would find there. Later, she herself took the flowers in her hands and arranged them in his *tilma* or mantle, telling him to show them only to the bishop. Encouraged by the words of the Virgin,

Juan Diego went directly to the bishop's residence. He had to wait a long time and was worried that others would want to see what he was hiding in his cloak. When he opened the *tilma* a little, one of the bystanders tried to touch the flowers, but in vain! They appeared to be embroidered, painted, or sewn on the cloth. This strange event was reported to the bishop, and he decided to receive Juan Diego, who was able finally to open the mantle and show the requested sign to the bishop. The roses and other sweet-smelling flowers fell to the ground and on the *tilma* there suddenly appeared the radiant image of the Virgin, offered for the veneration of those present who had fallen to their knees.

When Juan Diego returned home, after remaining for some days as guest of the bishop, he found that his uncle was completely cured. The Virgin had appeared also to Juan Bernardino, introducing herself with the name "Guadalupe" (*fifth apparition*).

As soon as the news of the prodigy had spread throughout the capital, the bishop's residence became a focal point for pilgrims who wanted to see the holy image, and so much so that he had to display it in the principal church of the city while the workmen were finishing the chapel requested by the Madonna, the one they called the first hermitage. On December 26 the *tilma* was transferred in solemn procession with the Spanish authorities and the Indian nobility all taking part. The image was transported by Franciscan friars under an elegant baldachino amidst crowds of jubilant natives.

The Guadalupan cult, in spite of the strong opposition of some of the missionaries, spread rapidly throughout the entire country, as we have been able to observe from our sources. Perhaps it was because of the hesitancy of some to admit the orthodoxy of the cult that Bishop Zumárraga left no official document, preferring to remain silent and let time clarify the facts.

Message of Our Lady

The Marian apparitions that took place on the hill of Tepeyac have rightly been called the "message of salvation." The Virgin speaks to Juan Diego and through him she wants to manifest herself to all her children who live in a state of oppression and frustration. Through Mary it is God himself who unites the people, speaks to them and pronounces words of hope. Although the Aztec gods are dead, the true God through whom one lives has not abandoned them. Rather, he entrusts their sufferings and their aspirations to his Mother. She is in fact also our Mother, our pious Mother. On Tepeyac the mystery of the divine and spiritual maternity of Mary shines forth; and, as we know, the mystery of the divine maternity is the mystery of the centrality of Christ. In this context one can see in the Marian manifestation at Tepeyac an echo of the manifestation of God to Moses in the burning bush. The lamentation of the Indians has reached the heart of God who, through Mary, announces and effects the promised liberation. Thus is established an authentically biblical rapport between the Christian faith and a new *mestizo* race of people. It is a new beginning, the basis of a life similar to that which God had stipulated in his covenant with Israel, making one people out of many tribes.

As the exodus of the Jews from Egypt had been the beginning of a new awareness of themselves as a people, so also the apparition of the Virgin of Tepeyac was the signal for a new culture. Mary gathered together a people and made them a Church. Her intervention makes one think spontaneously of the Visitation (Lk 1:39-56). Mary's visit to her cousin Elizabeth was a proclamation of Jesus. It was a communication of grace in which a communion between persons was deeply felt, especially in a time of need. Now Mary visits again, this time an entire people, and her purpose will be to lead them to a full realization of themselves as persons and to reveal to them their transcendent destiny (cf. *Marialis cultus*, n. 57).

Her task as Mother will be to point out to the Indians the true God. They would be asked to abandon idolatry but not to reject the substance of their native religiosity. They were simply to give it a new orientation. The newly proclaimed God bears names that are well known to the Aztecs. The Virgin does not announce the individual names of these divine realities, but only those which form the theological basis of the belief of the people. The Virgin of Guadalupe says that she is:

> the Mother of the one true God
> the Mother of the Giver of life
> the Mother of the Creator of mankind
> the Mother of the Lord of solidarity and unity
> the Mother of the Lord of heaven and earth.

In this way she makes reference to the very essence of God in his relationship to the world and to humankind. In this respect the Guadalupan event recovers part of the immense wealth of Aztec (Nahuatl) religiosity, giving it a fuller and more universal expression.

Juan Diego is likewise fully embraced by Mary in all his Indian reality; he is loved and exalted by her. He has been chosen to fulfill a mission. He is sent to liberate his people from hatred and animosity toward their conquerors, in order that a new people might rise up under the sign of unity, forgetting past tragedies and looking to the future that will be born of the union of the two races. This calls for the ability to live not in a state of fatal resignation or passive resentment, but with courageous and dynamic hope. The Virgin of Tepeyac is a model for all those who do not passively accept the adverse circumstances in their personal and social life, but proclaim with her that God "exalts the humble" and "casts down the mighty from their thrones."

As a mother, the Virgin wants to be present among her children permanently, to foster a dialogue, a communion, and to see realized the unity of believers. So she requests that there be erected in that place a shrine which will be a point of reference to which the people will be drawn to pray to the one true God proclaimed

by her. There she wants to be loved and invoked; there she wants
her children to learn how to trust her. Mary wants to show how
close God is to man in his concrete daily existence. She accompanies Juan Diego on the way; she is interested in what he does; she
comes to console him in his trials; she is close to anyone who no
longer has any hope.

The healing which God has prepared for his people is for the
whole person. This is shown in the healing of Juan Bernardino,
the uncle of Juan Diego. Sickness is one of the many afflictions
that hold man in bondage. The miraculous cure reminds us also
that the gift of the Virgin transcends every limit, and that the basis of salvation is always faith.

She seeks the good of her children; she wants them to grow
in faith. Mary asks her messenger to go to the bishop so that he
can authorize the construction of the little shrine she has requested.
She thus recognizes the authority of the Church and the role of
the spiritual guide of the people of God, a people that must learn
how to live the faith in a community of brothers and sisters as
children of one Father. Hence the Mexican bishops insisted in their
pastoral exhortation in 1978 that the only way to be brothers and
sisters of one another is to recognize that we all have the same
Father. At the end of the *Nican Mopohua* we already find ourselves
confronted by the reality of a new community reunited by the presence of Mary.

Theological insights

If we take into account the Guadalupan event from a strictly
theological point of view, we can describe it as evangelization by
means of words, symbols and miracles, not unlike Christ's own
means of evangelization. And, as with Christ, God is always at the
center.

There are numerous biblical references. The first mention of
the time and place of the apparitions introduces us to a *milieu* satu-

rated with the supernatural and divine: "It was very early on the Sabbath...." "Around the hill dawn was breaking." It is indicative that a supernatural manifestation should take place on a mountain, even a hill of modest height, because the summit of a mountain has always been seen as a point of contact with divinity. The time of day also has a symbolic value in the mentality of the natives: it refers to the "beginning," the birth of something new and great.

Attracted by the heavenly music—the song of the birds was a sign in the Aztec mentality, along with the presence of flowers, of a divine communication that was about to take place—Juan Diego raises his eyes to the summit of the hill and hears a voice calling him, calling his name, as had often happened in divine manifestations in the Bible (Gn 22:1; 1 S 3:4). On hearing his name, Juan Diego moves forward. He was in no way intimidated; rather, it seems he rejoiced at the presence of these supernatural signs and dares to walk in the direction from which they came. He felt himself to have entered the paradise of which his ancestors so often spoke, "a place in which flowers abound" and "that place from which all of us once came." Suddenly he finds himself face to face with the source of the voice: a Lady standing on the hillside and resplendent with light, something also typical of divine manifestations recorded in the Bible (see Ex 19:16-20, Ezk 1:5-28, Lk 2:8-14, Ac 2:1-4 and 9:1-19, Rv 21:9-27). The hill itself was a desolate piece of ground covered with cactus and thornbushes, but now it has become a place full of life. At this point words are spoken as the resplendent figure introduces herself as the ever Virgin Mary. From the very beginning the Church has proclaimed the perpetual virginity of Mary, based on the Gospels of Matthew (Mt 1:18-15) and Luke (Lk 1:26-38). In addition to this, Mary is full of grace and consequently shares in a singular way in the holiness of God. "Holy because of her union with the Incarnate Word, in an exclusive and personal way as his Mother; holy by her privileges, the gifts of grace which God bestowed on her since her immaculate conception; holy in the response she gave by preserving grace and practicing the virtues to perfection" (Mexican Episcopate, *La Presencia de Nuestra*

Señora de Guadalupe, 1978). All of the gifts, privileges and grandeur of the Virgin Mary have their roots in the fact that she is the
Mother of Jesus Christ, the Son of God made man.

The Virgin Mary does not mention the name of Jesus directly.
She speaks in the simple language of faith, as is used in the second
half of the *Ave Maria:* "Holy Mary, Mother of God, pray for us sin-
ners." It is clear to Juan Diego, however, that she is "the mother of
our Savior Jesus Christ," because he already knew the fundamental teaching of the catechism. The message of Guadalupe touches
the very heart of the revealed mystery: Mary of Guadalupe is the
Virgin Mother of God.

We have already mentioned the familiarity of the native Indians with the divine attributes of the Virgin. It is necessary to em-
phasize here that in ancient religions the expression "Mother of
God" or "our Mother" often indicated the feminine aspect of reality, but here the Virgin wants to make it clear that her primary
task is to make God known to the nations. She will do this through
the vocation which is proper to her: that of a most tender Mother
who keeps a protective watch over her children, not only those of
Mexico, but all who are devoted to her. The message of Guadalupe
is throughout a hymn of praise to the spiritual motherhood of Mary,
intoned by herself, as can be seen especially in the fourth apparition: "Am I not here, who am your Mother?" What she bears in
her womb, according to the symbolism and decorations on her
tunic, is the Son of God, but at the same time it symbolizes the
Mexican people.

At the very beginning the Virgin asks that a shrine be built
on the hill of Tepeyac. The idea of a shrine is a response to a very
profound religious need in human beings. Every group of people
has felt the need to find a place and consecrate it to the divinity
so that God may dwell therein (Ex 25:8). It was precisely to respond to this intimate need for contact with God that the Virgin
asked for a shrine where she could dispense her favors.

In this context of intercession for all the people, the figure of
Juan Diego also takes shape. He is the messenger used by the Ma-

donna: "Tell him [the bishop] that I sent you." Like a true prophet, Juan Diego is a servant prompt to obey, faithful to the command given in spite of his initial failure. He is the one who was chosen and he will not be replaced by someone better known, respected or honored. It is through his cooperation that the desire of the Virgin will be realized. As a man of faith, Juan Diego will not only be available but he will not try to benefit from the Virgin's power by asking of her that which is humanly impossible. The Virgin herself will appear to his uncle and cure him. Juan Bernardino will provide the other testimony of the event: Mary had revealed to him her title: "Guadalupe." Comforted by all this good news, Juan Diego does not hesitate for a moment but hastens to return a second time to the bishop with the sign the bishop had requested.

We should pause here to consider the importance of signs in the events of Guadalupe. First of all, the flowers which the Virgin herself arranged in Juan Diego's *tilma* after commanding him to pick them. They were roses and numerous other sweet-smelling flowers, sprinkled with dew, which had blossomed outside the proper season in an extraordinary way and in a place which normally abounds in rocks, thistles, thorns and cactus. The other sign is the image impressed on Juan Diego's *tilma* and venerated under the name revealed to Juan Bernardino: the "Perfect Virgin, Holy Mary of Guadalupe." This title has been amply investigated by scholars.

When the Madonna appeared to Juan Diego, the word "Guadalupe" already had a long history in its own right. Guadalupe was the name of a Spanish region located near Cáceres, in Estremadura, Spain, from which came the greater number of conquistadors and also the bishop of Mexico City, Fray Juan de Zumárraga. At the time of the conquest the shrine of Our Lady of Guadalupe in Estremadura was very popular and well-known. The term "Guadalupe" is a Spanish word of Arabic origin, but its meaning is obscure. Some scholars think that the literal meaning of the word is "river of light" or "river of love." Others have tried to interpret the word by using Nahuatl etymology, but this would result in distorting the original meaning. After all, the Virgin chose to identify herself with a title dear to the Spaniards. This sign definitely refers to the Virgin Mary of the Christian tradition.

For Juan Diego, the image on the *tilma* was a confirmation of his faith; for the bishop it was a sign that he should believe in the apparition; and for the Indians it was the work of a heavenly painter containing a message passed over inadvertently by the Spaniards. The fact is that while our culture concentrates on words, the Nahuatl culture responds to images. For us the image is perhaps a picture, a reproduction of reality, and is only secondarily a communication. But in producing their *amoxtli* or codices, the Indians did not intend to reproduce reality, but to communicate convictions in a picturesque way. Hence, the image, united to the narrative by a brother of the same race in the Nahuatl language and with a detailed symbolism, stimulated the conversion *en masse* of the Indians to the Queen of heaven.

Anthropological content

The Blessed Virgin chose as her interlocutor a "poor Indian." In comparison with the other individuals in the story, he is a person of prominence. In fact, the Madonna first addresses herself to him, and only later to the bishop.

Also, the moment chosen is significant. We read in *Nican Mopohua*: "Ten years after the fall of Mexico City, the arrows and shields were laid down." We have already seen that for the Aztecs war was an expression of their culture. After having lived as nomads, they became a warring people. For them war had both a social and a religious dimension (cf. the institution of the *guerra florida*, the flower war). Consequently, the end of war had great significance; it meant that they were approaching the end of their society, of their nation.

Later on, *Nican Mopohua* insists again on the fact that Juan Diego was a "poor Indian," which is an example of a grammatical use common among the Aztecs. Important realities are expressed with two words or with the repetition of words. For example, the world is expressed as "heaven and earth"; man, as "face and heart"; God, as "night and wind"; truth, as "flowers and song".

To the Indian it is given to grasp the truth, to grasp the divine event as "true," through flowers and song. The dignity of the Indian is emphasized by the name with which the Virgin calls him: "*Juantzin*" or "*Juandiegotzin*," normally translated into Spanish as *Juanito* or *Juandieguito*. But in Nahuatl the ending *-tzin* is used as a sign of reverence and respect. The diminutive form "*-ito*" is commonly used only with family and friends. In other languages and cultures we find the same usage.

The Virgin addresses the poor Indian as a person, a man, and for that reason she appears to him standing. The noble conquerors, be they Aztec, Mayan or Spaniards, always received their inferiors seated. Hence the nobility that Juan Diego sees in the Lady is not one of domination. The Indian recognizes in her a certain superiority, but he expresses it in a very familiar and affectionate manner, calling her "my child," "my little girl." In a climate of respect and gentility the conversation between "the smallest of her sons"—an expression referring to the humble condition in which the Indian finds himself—and the Virgin takes place. This is the typical cordiality of the Nahuatl language.

The "poor Indian," thus, becomes the witness to the Guadalupe event, its mediator. The Virgin asks the help of Juan Diego. After the failure of the first attempt, Juan Diego kneels at the feet of the bishop and weeping, repeats the request of the Madonna. In spite of everything, in the course of this dialogue rendered all the more difficult on account of Bishop Zumárraga's disbelief, the poor Indian still hopes against hope.

At the crucial moment of Juan Diego's mission—when he found it necessary to ask the Virgin for a sign—the sickness of his uncle intervened. This is decisive for understanding the meaning of the event. For the Aztecs and the Latin Americans in general an uncle has a social position of great importance. To call someone "uncle" was the greatest expression of respect that could be addressed to an adult. This is the key for understanding the region and the people. The gravity of the uncle's illness is a sign of the presence of something destructive within the social organization.

The sickness from which the uncle was dying was caused by contact with the Spaniards and was previously unknown to the natives. It represented all the calamities and afflictions that weigh heavily on an oppressed people. The Virgin of Guadalupe will take action concerning the illness of Juan Diego's uncle, attentive to the needs of this poor man, whose Mother she is. He is "under [her] shadow and protection." She has him in her care. For the Aztecs the person who has authority also has responsibility for the care of all things, great and small. The healing of the uncle is a sign of the redemption of the people from death. With the recovery of Juan Bernardino, the Guadalupan event reaches its apex. It began with a song, and now with the flowers the truth of the Virgin's promise becomes a fact.

In this case too the Virgin asks for Juan Diego's participation. He is to gather the flowers into a bundle there on the arid, cactus-covered hill, and bring them to her. On Tepeyac—which is another world—truth reigns supreme, as the Indian came to understand. In the flowers—and only later on the *tilma*—the sign of the Guadalupe event will remain forever, revealing the Virgin to Juan Diego, her trustworthy ambassador. He happily gathers the flowers into his *tilma*, confident this time of being able to successfully convince the bishop. If he accepts the flowers, he will also have to accept the truth of Guadalupe. This truth is now part of Juan Diego and nothing can ever take it from him. That is why the servants of the bishop could not take for themselves a single flower. It will be precisely when confronted by the flowers, even before seeing them, that the bishop will decide to support the project requested by the poor Indian. He will believe him after seeing the image imprinted on the *tilma*, and he will ask Juan Diego to indicate the place where the Madonna wants the shrine to be built. Everyone now defers to the Indian.

It seems fitting to conclude with the observations made recently by the Conference of Mexican Bishops concerning the anthropological aspect of the Guadalupe event. In the Pastoral Exhortation *La presencia* the bishops state that Juan Diego was determined not to let the affair pass, but to profit from the present and think about the future. He was determined to do all in his power not to sit on the sidelines waiting for others to do the work and assume the responsibility. He would be the master of his own destiny and, setting aside any vendetta, would strive to reach his objective, making use of truth and justice.

Symbolism of the image

To a people accustomed to communicate by means of painted symbols, Our Lady of Guadalupe provides an image that is as clear for the Indians in its symbolism as it is comprehensible to the missionaries. The cloth on which the image is impressed measures 170 by 140 cm. (5.5 ft. by 4.6 ft.). It is made in two parts united by a vertical seam made with thread of the same material. The measurements correspond to a *tilma* or mantle suited for a person of medium stature, e.g., 5' 6" tall. It was sewn with *maguey* thread, which is still used in Mexico today. The *tilma* worn by the natives fits the individual rather snugly. There are no signs of tearing or mending. It is extraordinary that it could still be intact today, because normally the material lasts at most 30 or 40 years. In the 19th century a concentrated solution of nitric acid was spilled on the upper right hand corner of the garment while a worker was polishing the edge of the silver frame. The material was not destroyed and the stain left by the acid gradually disappeared. In 1923 a terrorist exploded a bomb in front of the altar, a few feet from the image. A candelabra situated a short distance from the image was badly bent but the *tilma* suffered no damage at all.

The image can be understood to represent the Immaculate Conception or Mary's Assumption. Father Miguel Sánchez, who was the first to describe it, saw it as the Lady described in the Book of Revelation, where it speaks of a pregnant woman crowned with stars (Rv 12:1-7). She is standing on what appears to be a half-moon, although it can also be seen as a comet, the symbol of the Aztec god Quetzalcoátl. Her head is inclined devoutly a bit to the right and her hands are joined at the height of her cincture. Her face is extremely beautiful, serious, noble and somewhat dark complexioned (*morena*). The image is fully illuminated with the rays of the sun. The Lady wears a rose-colored tunic that extends below the ankles and is covered with floral designs in gold thread which stand out in relief on the surface of the tunic. The floral designs are of flowers familiar to the Aztecs and at her neck she wears a jade brooch, the Aztec symbol of life, in the middle of which is a Christian cross, although it could also be a quincunx, which is the symbol of the Aztec god Quetzalcoátl. (Jade was a symbol of life for the Aztecs, and when a woman gave birth to a son, the husband gave her a gift made of jade.) Under the rose-colored tunic one can detect a white undergarment. The mantle is sky-blue and it descends from her head to her feet, leaving her face visible. It is bordered in gold and sprinkled with golden stars. The figure of the Lady is held up by the two arms of an angel, who "seems very happy to support on his wings the Queen of heaven" (from the document *In Tilmatzintli*). The image does not conform to the European style of painting in the 16th century. As is evident from what we have said thus far, there are numerous elements that relate directly to Aztec religion and culture, although some experts have stated that the Lady is dressed in the manner of young Jewish women at the time of Christ.

One expert observed that it is certain that the Lady came down from heaven because the rays from the sun surround her, piercing the clouds; the stars adorn her mantle; and her feet rest on the crescent of the moon. She comes from the east and puts the cosmos in order; otherwise it would not be possible that the stars would be properly paired. She comes to put an end to the imagined astral struggle because the Virgin is able to keep them in perfect equilibrium. The heavenly bodies are not gods, but creatures subject to a superior order. The "Fifth Sun" of the Aztecs does not die, but the Virgin of Guadalupe announces a new Sun of justice and holiness: Christ. From the position of her hands and the inclined head, we can conclude that the Virgin is reverencing someone higher than herself. Her blue mantle, the symbol of heaven and of power, covers her completely and is of the same color worn by the Aztec kings (tlatoani), so she is called "Empress of the Americas."

On the other hand, the Lady also belongs to the earth, as indicated by the color of her tunic: rose-colored like the dawn in the Valley of Mexico. The tunic is covered with sketches of Aztec flowers. The hill of Tepeyac is transformed from an arid and rocky place to a green and flowered area, thanks to a beneficent influx from heaven, as is represented by the mantle. The Virgin and Mother, Queen of heaven and earth, is showing reverence to a superior being, to her Creator, as is indicated by the position of her hands and her inclined head.

Numerous in-depth scientific studies have been made of the image, among them that of the 1938 Nobel Prize-winner for chemistry, Richard Kuhn. In 1936, he examined some fibers from the tilma in order to analyze their resistance to dust. He came to the conclusion that the colors of the image did not come from animal, vegetable or mineral elements. We should keep in mind that some details of the image may have been added or retouched at the beginning of the 17th century. Such at least is the opinion of Father Valerio Maccagnan, author of the article "Guadalupe" in Nuovo Dizionario di Mariologia. Scientists from NASA have also studied the image by using infra-red rays and have formulated their hypotheses:

1. The original figure comprises the rose-colored tunic, the sky-blue mantle, the hands, the face and the right foot. The type of color pigment used for these parts is inexplicable; likewise unexplained is the duration of the luminosity of the colors, lasting for a period of 450 years, taking into account the conditions in which the image was preserved for more than a century, exposed to high humidity in the small chapel, to the smoke of candles, and

the devotion of the faithful, who were able to approach it, touch it and kiss it. Since 1647 the image has been in a frame and protected by a glass.

2. The original image does not give any indication of fading or of cracking in any area of the *tilma*. Not having been treated with any preservative, the image should not have lasted 100 years, but it has lasted more than 450 years. The fact that the *tilma* was not treated in any way before its use and was kept in such inadequate conditions, makes it inexplicable in the light of modern scientific knowledge why the colors are still so visible and brilliant. There are no traces of an outline; nor is there in the history of painting an image similarly produced. It is something unheard of in the art world, inexplicable and unrepeatable.

3. It is possible that as early as the 16th century human hands made the first modifications to the *tilma*. In the 17th century, after the terrible flood of 1629, the image was transferred to the cathedral in Mexico City and perhaps it was necessary to restore the bottom part of the *tilma* damaged by the water and darkened by dust and the smoke from candles. In 1980, Rodrigo Franyutti, an expert examined photographs of the image and stated that the face of the image seems to have been retouched during the period from 1926 to 1930 because today the image seems more obscure and the lines coarser.

There are others, however, who say that the image has not undergone any modification, and they point to a study published in 1945 which confirms that the technique that produced the original image of Guadalupe, unlike the codex possessed by Father Maccagnan, is not comparable to any of the great masterpieces. The image in Father Maccagnan's possession is slightly different and is thought to be the work of the talented Indian painter Marcos Cipac whose major works were done between 1550 and 1570. Cipac was thought to be the author of the original image by the Franciscan Provincial, Bustamante, who declared this in his homily at the time of the transfer of the image from the primitive shrine to the Basilica built at the order of Bishop Montúfar. As we saw earlier, nothing ever came of his claim.

CHAPTER THREE

Juan Diego

FOR THE APPARITIONS to be recognized as such, it is necessary to examine the person who received them, the manner in which they were verified, and the effects they produced. If the person receiving the visions is a person of outstanding virtue; if everything that occurs is for the glory of God and there is nothing to the contrary; if after receiving the visions the person thus favored by God grows in humility and the other Christian virtues; it is virtually impossible to doubt in any way the supernatural and divine character of the apparitions.

Father E. Anticoli, S.J., in his *Historia de la Aparición* (1979), shows that in the Guadalupan apparitions the three conditions listed by the Congregation of Rites have been verified. In fact, Juan Diego, though he was the only witness of the event, was a man who could be believed. He had enjoyed a reputation for holiness even before the apparitions. Judging from the questions asked of him by Bishop Zumárraga and from the answers that he gave, signs of an authentic supernatural apparition can be shown to be present. And as regards the effects, the fact that Juan Diego had left his home and property to dedicate himself full time to the service of the Virgin, living a life of penance and prayer, is a confirmation of his holiness of life. Because of his reputation for holiness, he was pictured next to the Madonna in the ancient oratory of Cuauhtitlán.

The Church maintains that the criteria for the authenticity

of apparitions should be the conformity of the life of the visionary with the Church's moral teaching and the truthfulness of his or her statements. The visionary should be a person who is well balanced, open and humble. As regards the signs, more importance is given to healings than to spectacular and extraordinary manifestations such as luminous phenomena, distinct aromas, and other sensate changes. The principal sign of authenticity, therefore, is the fruits produced.

Studies on Juan Diego

It is only in recent times that Juan Diego has become an object of investigation, with the opening of the cause for his beatification (1984), which culminated with the decree *Exaltavit humiles*, promulgated by Pope John Paul II on May 6, 1990. Permission was granted for a liturgical memorial in honor of Blessed Juan Diego Cuauhtlotatzin on December 9, the date of the first apparition. This explains the importance given to the declaration of the authenticity of his sanctity rather than to his historicity.

The study that has tried especially to offer a solidly documented basis for the historicity of Juan Diego is perhaps the one by Lauro López Beltrán, presented in 1977 at the Second National Meeting on Guadalupe. The author maintained that up until that time interested parties were more preoccupied with the historicity of the apparitions than with that of Juan Diego. This enabled the persons who were opposed to the apparitions to insist that Our Lady of Guadalupe was a myth.

To the supposed lack of historical data sufficient for canonization, López Beltrán replied by listing the sources, which he subdivided into those coming from an Indian and those from a Spanish context, both direct and indirect, which allude to the Guadalupan incident and consequently to the existence of Juan Diego. Among the direct indigenous documents, in addition to *Nican Mopohua* and *Nican Motecpana*, he notes *Testamento de Juana*

Martín (1559), originally written in Nahuatl and found under *Documentos Guadalupanos* in the New York Public Library; a manuscript in Nahuatl called *Ixtlamatque Tlaxcaltecatl* (to be found in the Historical Archives of the National Institute of Anthropology and History, Mexico City) in which the date of Juan Diego's death is given as 1548; and the *Testamento de Juan Diego*, found by Lorenzo Boturini Benaduci but no longer available, though it is listed in the inventory of documents compiled by the Italian historian. The original of this inventory can be found in the Library of the National Institute of Anthropology and History in Mexico City. As regards Spanish documents, López Beltrán lists *Informaciones de 1666*, which drew on depositions by Indians and Spaniards concerning the life and virtues, the reputation for holiness and the cult of Juan Diego.

Next, Beltrán outlines the biography of Juan Diego whom he calls "our candidate for the altars." In his general bibliography from the 16th to the 20th centuries, one will find only the principal authors who have written about the apparitions of Guadalupe, such as Miguel Sánchez, Luis Becerra Tanco, Francisco de Florencia and Carlos de Sigüenza y Góngora. He closes his review with the desire that Juan Diego may soon be raised to the honors of the altar, since the Archbishop of Mexico City, Ernesto Corripio Ahumada, has said that "his canonization is possible."

Some years later (in 1981) a study appeared in a volume with various appendices. It contained a collection of miracles attributed to Juan Diego; an article on the various places thought to contain his mortal remains; and some suggestions for the formation of an historical commission with a view to his beatification. In 1940 there actually was a commission set up to collect the documentation, but its work was judged to be insufficient by the higher authorities in Rome.

If we move now to take into consideration the study presented by Manuel Rángel Camacho in 1981 and later amplified (1984), we can say that it was this author's intention to prove that Juan Diego's reputation for holiness has existed since the second half of the 16th century. The author thus reviews texts and homilies that refer to Juan Diego, beginning with the oldest. He portrays Juan Diego as an ideal model, possessing all the virtues and worthy to be compared to the outstanding examples in biblical history. From Sánchez, who calls him "a new Adam," superior to the first one, there pass before our eyes parallel examples of the most outstanding figures such as Jacob, Moses and Tobias, which appear to us today to be highly exaggerated. Many sermons are reported in which the preachers multiply the praises of Juan Diego, as in the second century of the apparitions, when he was called "the symbol of the human grandeur of the Indians."

The book, *Juan Diego, el vidente del Tepeyac*, gathers together what the various authors, especially historians, have written about Juan Diego. First of all, the biographical data is presented, giving a great deal of space to the virtues of the messenger of Our Lady and offering to historians a basis for their depositions at the process for his canonization. Then follows a brief anthology of studies, some of which are of a certain historical interest, such as those of Ramón Sánchez Flores, who tries to place Juan Diego in the wider context of his family and contemporaries, and like the article by Alberto Fragoso Castañares, the archivist of Cuauhtitlán (the birthplace of Juan Diego), which was published in the official organ of the Center of Guadalupan Studies. Another article of interest is one on the "Figure of the Lay Person in Evangelization" by Alfonso Alcalá Alvarado, who attempts a spiritual portrait of Juan Diego drawn from the three principal sources: *Nican Mopohua*, *Nican Motecpana* and *Informaciones de 1666*. There is also a detailed study of the last-mentioned work by Ana María Sada Lambretón, pulling together the data that emerges from the life, the virtues, the reputation for sanctity and the cult of Juan Diego.

Biographical data

Various sources provide us with biographical data concerning Juan Diego. The place of his birth is certain: the region of

Tlatacác in the province of Cuauhtitlán, today at the gates of Mexico City. As to the date of birth, while some authors speak vaguely about the years prior to the coming of the Spaniards, others, like Fernando de Alva and Luis Becerra Tanco, are more precise and give the year 1474. There is no doubt that Juan Diego came from the Chichimeca tribe and belonged to the middle class (*macehuales*), and that he was a farmer and small landowner. Juan Diego's Aztec name, as we pointed out earlier, was Cuauhtlotatzin, meaning "the one who speaks like an eagle."

His parents' names are unknown and nothing has come down to us about Juan Diego's infancy or youth. His livelihood came from his work in the fields and later from his proficiency at making mats and furniture from reeds that were plentiful along the shores of Lake Texcoco. Cuauhtitlán at that time was composed of several *calpullis* or large houses inhabited by members of the same family according to the traditional hierarchy. The ancient testimony states that Juan Diego was a *macehual* or man from the middle class. He owned a small plot of land and a house that he inherited from his father. Modern investigations reveal that he was of the upper middle class, with greater than average possessions, and therefore the emphasis on his poverty (that he was a poor Indian) should be understood in the sense that he lived an evangelical or voluntary poverty of spirit.

The reference to the presence of his uncle, Juan Bernardino, in Juan Diego's house is found in the *Nican Mopohua* and the testimony of the natives contained in *Informaciones de 1666*. But it should be noted that among the Aztecs the authority of an uncle had the same force as that of a parent, so it is not surprising that Juan Bernardino was the object of his nephew's great care and attention. Juan Diego surely could have counted on the help of other relatives living in the same region.

On reaching maturity, Juan Diego married Malitzin, a young woman from Tulpetlac, which was some kilometers distance from Cuauhtitlán. That particular region was among the first to be evangelized, a few years after the arrival of the Spaniards, by the early Franciscan missionaries, among whom was Pedro de Gante, who arrived in 1523 and settled at Texcoco, the capital of the Chichimecas. In 1524 the group of twelve Franciscan friars arrived. Cuauhtlotatzin together with his wife and uncle were among the first to be baptized receiving the new names, Juan Diego, María Lucía and Juan Bernardino. It was most probably Fray Toribio de Benavente (better known as Motolinía) who administered the sacrament to the young married couple and Juan Diego's uncle.

Juan Diego distinguished himself among the converts by his conscientious attendance at catechism classes and the reception of the sacraments, without regard for the sacrifices involved. In the very early hours of the morning he would set out for Santiago de Tlatelolco, where the catechism lessons for the Indians were held. His lifestyle was a source of edification for many. The premature death of María Lucía in 1529 left Juan Diego a widower at the age of 55. There is no record of any children born into this marriage. From that time on, Juan Diego's life was more and more centered on God, and his witness to the faith gave his fellow-citizens some hope that soon their oppression would be lifted. After the death of his wife, Juan Diego moved to Tulpetlac to live with his uncle, Juan Bernardino, and it was in his house that the fifth apparition of the Virgin occurred.

The extraordinary event that Juan Diego experienced at Tepeyac took place in a life already transformed by the grace of baptism and would prompt him eventually to leave his uncle in order to move into a little hut that Bishop Zumárraga had commanded to be built, next to the little shrine erected in honor of the Virgin Mary. Here Juan Diego lived for about seventeen years in prayer and penance, performing the humble function of a sacristan, without ever failing in his duties. By his humility and purity of heart he gave testimony to what the Virgin Mary had done for him and will do for all those who turn to her with childlike affection.

His reputation for holiness which was already well known among his neighbors increased greatly during the years that Juan Diego spent in retirement at Tepeyac. He greatly edified all those who visited the place of the apparition. Many of the pilgrims asked Juan Diego to pray for their spiritual and temporal needs. His death from the plague occurred in 1548 when he was 74, four years following the death of his uncle, and a few months after that of Bishop Zumárraga. He was buried in the chapel of the Madonna, next to his uncle. López Beltran holds that his remains were later transferred from place to place as the image of the Virgin was also moved: in 1556 to the chapel at Montúfar, in 1622 to the new church, in 1647 back to the chapel at Montúfar which had been restored by Lasso de la Vega, and finally in 1649 to what was to become the sacristy of the Church of the Indians, opened in 1694. From that point on nothing further is known of what happened to his mortal remains.

The devout Guadalupan

The biography of Juan Diego shows us that the extraordinary experience at Tepeyac was inserted into a life that was already replete with Christian values and Marian piety. The Franciscan friars were well known as promoters of Marian devotion and very likely they would already have introduced the traditional Saturday Mass in her honor. In all probability at dawn on December 9, 1531 Juan Diego was on his way to Tepeyac, possibly to honor the Virgin Mary. We like to think that he had already received and was continuing to increase his Marian formation within his general Christian formation. This also would have been a preparation for the supernatural manifestation on Tepeyac. To this newly converted Indian the Tepeyac region will seem transformed, it will be a new world. There he will hear his name pronounced with love and respect; there he will receive his mission, which he will accept with all humility, faith and availability; there he will be gratified at the sign of blooming flowers, the prelude to the springtime of salvation.

Juan Diego had already understood that the cult to Mary

could not be limited to prayer and invocation, but must extend to imitation. Our Lady of Guadalupe, who appeared to Juan Diego clothed in the sun, not only announced that she is our spiritual mother, but invited him to open his heart to the salvific work of Christ. He accepted the role of ambassador with a sense of responsibility and feelings of gratitude, humility and availability, giving expression to his decision as a free man fully conscious of what he was doing. First of all, he placed himself at the service of others; not only of his uncle but also of so many needy Indians, especially during the years that he was definitively in charge of caring for the little chapel. His life of voluntary poverty, lived in humility, interior silence, and recollection, nourished by purity of heart and a new spirit, was the best catechesis of the devout Guadalupan. As Mary had abandoned herself in total faith to the Lord, who called her and assigned her to a mission, in the same way Juan Diego yielded to others who shared his faith, which was nourished by the sacraments of penance and the Eucharist. Mary wants us to unite ourselves to her intentions in order that we might love her Son better in our sisters and brothers. She asks us to serve Him with infinite respect in our neighbor and, like herself, to see Him present in every man and woman.

Juan Diego knew how to blend faith and life, a tender personal love for Mary as his Mother and a concrete sense of solidarity, showing that he had accepted Mary as his Mother and the Mother of all believers. Taking upon himself the attitude of Mary, who exercises her maternity not as a privilege but as a service, Juan Diego expressed his Marian devotion by goodness and availability to his fellow-citizens. Following Mary's example, Juan Diego disposes himself to be of evangelical service to all. He still teaches us how to understand the will of Mary who, with maternal love, takes care of the brethren of her Son. Like her, Juan Diego is willing to walk in the obscurity of faith and to discover, moment by moment, the steps he is to take. He takes upon himself the asceticism that every Christian ought to embrace in order to arrive at the summit of the mount; in other words, he put aside the old man in order to be clothed with the new (Col 3:9-10). The image of Mary, permanently impressed on the *tilma*, signifies her constant intercession for believers that the pathway of grace may be manifested in them. In the presence of Mary, God's way merges with that of man. In Christ is the fullness of all creation, and Mary brings it all back to him: *"Ad Jesum per Mariam."*

Holiness of life

The experience at Tepeyac resulted in a change of life for Juan Diego. In order to understand how it came about it is necessary to discuss in greater detail the virtues that he practiced. These are what primarily gave him the reputation for holiness, especially after the apparitions.

The principal sources for this information are:

Nican Mopohua, the account of the apparitions of the Blessed
   Virgin Mary to Juan Diego;
Nican Motecpana, description of the first miracles, written perhaps by Fernando de Alva Ixtlilxóchitl and published at
   the same time as *Nican Mopohua* in the Nahuatl language.
Informaciones de 1666, along with a collection of testimonies
   to the tradition by those who had known Juan Diego.

We shall first consider the theological virtues of faith, hope and charity. Faith and filial abandonment emerge from the account of the apparitions. Juan Diego immediately believes that his uncle will be cured; he goes to the summit of the hill to gather flowers, although it is not the place or the season for flowers, because he is certain that the Virgin will keep her word. It is also important to note that after his conversion, Juan Diego never had any doubts concerning the truth of the Catholic faith.

Confronted by the skepticism of the bishop, Juan Diego places all his trust in the Virgin Mary, conscious of his own poverty and littleness. Trusting firmly in the protection of the Lady from heaven, he endures fatigue and humiliations as he perseveres in the service of the Virgin Mary until the hour of his death. After the apparitions, he has no other preoccupation than eternal salvation, and prayer is the motivating power of his hope and the expression of his desire for perfect union with the Lord.

Effectively achieving total denial of self in the hidden life, Juan Diego united love of God to love of neighbor, regardless of the sacrifice. His love of neighbor was manifested in the promptness with which he attended to the needs of his uncle and the zeal with which he prayed for his brethren during the time he lived at the little chapel at Tepeyac, after giving up everything that he possessed in order to live voluntary evangelical poverty.

He was a model of the virtuous life even before the apparitions: an integrated man, peaceful, honest, God-fearing, mortified, serene in every circumstance, a friend to those who walk on the right path. He was a model to those around him and a first apostle to the New World. Those who knew him were inspired by him to praise God, and parents encouraged their children to be like Juan Diego.

The witnesses who were questioned in 1666 unanimously agreed that he was a saint. They emphasized that he subjected himself to fasting and corporal penance and that he had great devotion to the Eucharist. With the permission of the bishop, he was able to receive Communion three times a week, something exceptional in those days and a proof of his purity of heart. The witnesses also testified to his humility, faith, apostolic zeal and love of prayer. He frequently retired to solitude in order to pray and meditate on the graces and benefits he had received.

His faithfulness in attending the religious instruction given by the Franciscan friars was remembered as something worthy of note. Juan Diego would traverse great distances in spite of the fatigue and sacrifice in order to attend the catechism lessons. This was seen as a clear sign of his fundamental option for the Lord and his joy at being a member of the Church, even in the days when he was a recent convert. He had a great eagerness to know the content of Christian belief.

The virtue that was most perceptible to his contemporaries was the virtue of humility. Juan Diego had a low opinion of himself, and even after having received such extraordinary favors he never became proud or boastful but referred everything to God. His humility was tested, as were his other virtues, in an incident described by Francisco de Florencia. Having arrived late for catechism and the Mass following his first visit to the bishop's palace, he submitted himself without any excuse to the penitential act of the discipline, as was then the custom. This testimony was given by Father Chauvet, the provincial superior of the Franciscans. Later on, while in service at the little chapel at Tepeyac, he was always under the authority of the chaplain and performed the most humble and heavy tasks.

Finally, Juan Diego was an obedient man. He kept firmly in mind the commandments of the Lord and walked always in accordance with them. Ever heeding the wishes of God, he offered to Him the sacrifice of a pure conscience and a soul eminently disposed to heed the word of the Lord.

Exultavit humiles

Juan Diego's reputation for holiness has remained constant since the first half of the 16th century. Even before the decree *Caelestis Hierusalem Cives* was issued by Pope Urban VIII in 1634, he was venerated by the people to such an extent that in some paintings he was pictured with a halo. This is the testimony of numerous persons who contributed to the *Informaciones de 1666*. This was especially the case with individual churches in Mexico in times of great religious fervor. In the work, *Lienzo de Cuauhquechollan*, there are several illustrations pertaining to the life of Juan Diego and the apparitions of the Virgin Mary. One of the illustrations shows Juan Diego displaying his *tilma* with the image on it to the kneeling bishop. Another representation is of Juan Diego in glory, speaking with his wife María Lucía, and at the side is a drawing of Our Lady of Guadalupe. In yet another illustration Juan Diego is pictured in a halo of light, indicating his holiness. An indication that there was a cult to Juan Diego is demonstrated by the existence of a small shrine at the site of his former home at Tulpetlac. All of the foregoing suffices to demonstrate that the sanctity of Juan Diego merited for him the veneration of the people and something of a cult in his honor.

In compliance with the decree issued by Pope Urban VIII, the remains of Juan Diego were hidden in order to suppress any public veneration, which was otherwise getting to be uncontrollable. In recent times, however, Pope John Paul II on May 6, 1990 gave permission for the liturgical celebration of the memorial of Blessed Juan Diego on December 9, the day of the first apparition. Thus the cult of Juan Diego has been officially re-established.

In order to verify the reputation for the holiness of Juan Diego, work was begun in 1987 for the composition of the *Positio super fama sanctitatis, virtutibus et cultu ab immemorabili,* authorized by the Congregation for the Causes of Saints. The emphasis was centered on the life and virtues of Juan Diego, considered as much as possible apart from the apparitions of Our Lady of Guadalupe. By means of solid documentation the study set out to demonstrate that because of his own personal merits alone as a Christian, Juan Diego deserved to be declared a saint of the Church.

Regarding the documents collected for the *Positio,* we may note some new material from the study of López Beltrán, to which we have already referred. For example, the narrative entitled *Tres Conquistadores y Pobladores de la Nueva España* cites the Guadalupan event, giving the names of the protagonists and the dates. It describes Juan Diego as: "an Indian from San Juanito," confirming what was handed down in the oral tradition, namely, that at the time of the apparition Juan Diego was coming from Tulpetlac, which is next to San Juanito. It also states that that region belonged to the religious jurisdiction of Tlatelolco, to which Juan Diego belonged at the time of the apparitions. Among the documents of Spanish origin there is a defense of the virginity of Juan Diego, written by Lorenzo Boturini Benaduci. A witness at the diocesan process, Joel Romero Salinas, found in the Archives of the Indies at Seville (Spain), an entry by Lorenzo Benaduci which states: "I made a defense of the virginity of Juan Diego so that he would not be deprived of such a singular glory and to do what I could to confront those Indians who tried to prove that they were direct descendants of the visionary." This idea most probably came from the *Testamento de Juana Martín* (1559), which affirms that Juan Diego died a virgin.

Proof of the Indian name of Juan Diego can be found in the National Library in Paris in the volume, *Tira de Tepechpan* (1596), written in Nahuatl. It contains a picture of an eagle holding in its beak a turquoise scroll. Since the Indians used the color blue for anything relating to divinity, one could translate the picture to mean "the eagle that speaks exalted things." Moreover, one could see at the bottom of the drawing persons taking part in a procession. A cross, banners and a man wearing a miter can all be identified. Presumably this is a sketch of the procession in which on December 26, 1531, the image was transported to the little chapel which Bishop Juan de Zumárraga had commanded to be built. Also cited was the *Informaciones Guadalupanas* (1798-99) in which a fellow-citizen of Juan Diego promoted the construction of a shrine at Cuauhtitlán, where Juan Diego had lived.

Sent to the Congregation for the Causes of Saints in 1990, the *Positio* at first passed the examination of the experts, who judged that the historical basis for the declaration of sanctity, the cult from time immemorial, and the practice of the virtues to a heroic degree was valid. Theologians made the same positive assessment, and Pope John Paul II recognized the validity of the Guadalupan tradition. The ceremony of beatification took place in the new Basilica of Our Lady of Guadalupe in Mexico City on May 6, 1990.

In his homily the Holy Father proclaimed Juan Diego "an advocate and protector of the Indians" and proposed him as a model for the laity:

"The recognition of the centuries-old cult given to Juan Diego is of particular importance. It is a call to all the faithful lay persons of this nation to fulfill their responsibility in the transmission of the Gospel message and in the witness of a living and operative faith in the ambit of Mexican society."

CHAPTER FOUR

Continuity of the Tradition

THE MADONNA OF GUADALUPE was extremely intent on the implantation of the Church in the Aztec world. It is not difficult to see the reason for these conversions. We read in the *Nican Mopohua* that the Indians recognized in time the divine character (literally, "the coming of God") of the image of one of their own imprinted on the *tilma*. The message of Guadalupe is directed principally—though not exclusively—to the poor. It incarnates the faith in a world of the poor who are to become its subjects as well as its recipients. The experience of Juan Diego demonstrates this very well. Mary is the evangelizer who brings Christ. She announces a new epoch, a new way of life. Men will become brothers; they will share in the life that Christ gives us, forming a community, a new reconciled people. The Virgin Mary of Guadalupe brings with her a loving embrace for all her devoted children, and at the same time manifests God's clear preferential option for the poor and the marginalized. Her dialogue begins, in fact, with an Indian of humble condition and her center of irradiation will be Tepeyac, on the periphery of Mexico City, among the simple people, the populace, the least, the abandoned. We should not forget that for the dispersed and disoriented tribes of Mexico, Mary presented herself as a link in the chain of religious and national unity. Through the evangelical work of Mary, God will restore dignity to an entire people. Hence, we could consider the experience of Juan Diego as a paradigm of Mary's evangelical activity

which splendidly illumines the dawn of the ecclesiastical history
of the Latin American people.

It now remains for us to examine the continuity of the
Guadalupan tradition, concentrating especially on the 16th century, but without failing to acknowledge Guadalupan devotion in
our own day. In doing so, we also want to present the opinion of
those who are opposed to Guadalupe, e.g., Bustamante and
O'Gorman, whose ideas do not have to be totally rejected, even if
theirs is only a partial reading of the facts and is based on a prefab-
ricated hypothesis to justify their position.

Three viewpoints

The oral and written tradition of the Guadalupe event is
based on Spanish and Indian sources whose historical veracity is
in part disputed, resulting in an ongoing controversy, especially
between the *apparitionists* and the *anti-apparitionists*, namely, those
who maintain that the appearance of the Virgin Mary on Tepeyac
was an authentic historical event and those who deny it.

The apparitionists have successfully proven the historical existence of the *cult* of the Virgin of Tepeyac before the publication
of the works of Miguel Sánchez (1648) and Luis Lasso de la Vega
(1649). The controversy between Montúfar and Bustamante leaves
no doubt concerning the existence of the cult since the middle of
the 16th century, a cult which even today is well established in
every region of the country. The same thing can be said of the reg-
istration of the miracles which the Virgin worked on behalf of the
Indians and the Spaniards. Now, the cult and the testimony of the
miracles have been registered in documents that are authentically
historical, but they cannot prove the historicity of the apparitions.
In fact, in these documents we do not find any references to the
protagonists of the apparitions. For that reason, Joaquín García
Icazbalceta maintained that there are no references to Juan Diego
and Juan Bernardino until 1648.

The research on the proofs of the historical authenticity of the apparitions began probably in the 16th century, with meager results for those who had hoped to find testimony from the first bishop of Mexico concerning his participation in the events between December 9 and 12 or the procession on December 26 of the same year to the newly-built shrine at Tepeyac. Nevertheless, thanks to the work of the experts, an interesting collection of documents has come to light, such as the *Collección Boturini* (1746), the *Monumentos Guadalupanos* of José Fernando Ramírez, and the *Tesoro Guadalupano* of Fortino Hipólito Vera. Other sources, coming especially from an Indian context, were saved and copied because of references to Our Lady of Guadalupe.

If, moreover, we take into consideration the entire collection of available documents coming from Indian or Spanish sources, we can subdivide them into *direct* and *indirect*. Only a limited number of the former, however, were redacted with the primary intention of providing information about the Virgin and the shrine of Guadalupe, or else they make no mention of it because they did not think it was necessary.

Two eminent writers, Juan Bautista Muñoz (1794) and Joaquín García Icazbalceta (1883) deny the historical basis of the Guadalupan tradition. On the contrary, the apparitionists accept the tradition, including the reference to the miraculous impression of the image on the *tilma* of Juan Diego. For them the Guadalupan image itself is an historical proof. According to the apparitionist writers, the oral tradition can be accepted as an historical fact if it fulfills certain conditions; it must be "antique, constant, ample and not subject to controversies." The decisive arguments of the apparitionists focus on the content of the message, private revelation which does not contradict biblical revelation, holiness of life in the visionary, the fruit of conversion, faith in the Virgin Mary, and miracles obtained through her intercession. The popular devotion remains active, even though Guadalupe is not a dogma. The historicity derives from the acceptance of the account through faith.

In the middle of the 16th century the Franciscan Provincial, Fray Francisco Bustamante, declared that the Guadalupan devotion was "without any solid basis" and was, in fact, dangerous; and anyone who states that miracles can be worked by the image "painted by the Indian, Marcos Cipac," should be punished with flogging. We should not forget that a considerable number of missionaries did not approve of the cult of Tepeyac, which contradicted their principles and methods. The Franciscans in particular had noticed in the Indians a deep-seated tendency to idolatry. Consequently, they adopted as a practical norm never to approve the cult of any particular image or any shrine or sanctuary. The historians and authors of the Order, both those who mentioned the cult of Guadalupe and those who passed over it in silence, considered it ambiguous and saw it as a dangerous syncretism or even a form of idolatry under the appearance of a Christian cult. In his work, written between 1547 and 1570, Sahagún admitted that Indians came from great distances to honor the Virgin of Guadalupe but he believed that the cult was suspect. It is possible that the Indians were in reality paying homage to the pagan goddess Tonantzín who had been venerated previously on the hill of Tepeyac. Nevertheless, it was not until the end of the 18th century that the Guadalupan tradition was contested in Mexico or elsewhere.

The dissertation by the Spanish historian, Juan Bautista Muñoz, was first read in 1794 but was not published until 1817. When it did, he burst upon the scene like a thunderbolt. The principal, if not the only, argument put forward by Muñoz is the "argument of silence." He maintained that there was not the slightest hint of the apparitions prior to 1648. Therefore, the Guadalupan episode was invented by Sánchez. The testimony of Indians was looked on with disdain, and no weight was given to the declaration of Sigüenza y Góngora or to the contents of *Informaciones de 1666*, although it was impossible to deny the antiquity of the cult or the oral tradition.

In 1888 *Información que el Arzobispo don fray Alonso de*

*Montúfar mandó practicar con motivo de un sermón que en la fiesta de
la Natividad de Nuestra Señora (8 septiembre de 1556) predicó... el
Provincial fray Francisco de Bustamante acerca de la devoción y culto
de Nuestra Señora de Guadalupe* was published in Spain. Two years
later a Mexican edition was released. The document was originally
published at the behest of the archbishop of Mexico City, Alonso
de Montúfar (1498-1573) and it dealt with a sermon preached by
the Provincial of the Franciscans, Fray Francisco de Bustamante.
The content of the document is preceded by a note from the editors to the effect that their intention in publishing the work was
to prove that the argument in question was not about the apparition of 1531. Neither the two preachers nor the witnesses made
any mention of it; they limited their discussion to a little chapel
that had been dedicated to the Madonna.

Another important phase in the history of those who rejected
the apparitions was the publication in 1896 of *Carta sobre el origen
de la imagen de Guadalupe*. This was done without the permission
of the author, who had written it privately to the Archbishop of
Mexico City in 1883. In the letter the famous Mexican Catholic
writer, Joaquín García Icazbalceta, sees in the sermon by Francisco
de Bustamante a clear denial of the supernatural origin of the image. He thus placed himself in line with the editors of *Información
por el sermón de 1556*, and he once again emphasized the argument
of silence, which was evident in the case of Muñoz. The letter by
Icazbalceta became the strongest argument for the anti-
apparitionists from the point of view of the historiographers because of the seriousness with which he took up the argument and
because of the solid reputation of the author. For Icazbalceta the
principal problem for the historian was not the lack of belief in
the apparition of Our Lady, but the lack of contemporary historical witnesses to the fact. The absence of any historical references
to Juan Diego, Juan Bernardino and the apparitions at Tepeyac
before the publication of the books by Miguel Sánchez and Lasso
de la Vega became the *dictum* for the historians who then became
interested in the argument.

In the 20th century the discussion was resumed by Francisco de la Maza, who, in a book published for the first time in 1933, denied the credibility of the apparition and explained the origin of the image of the Virgin with the reproduction of a likeness of Our Lady of Guadalupe of Estremadura in Spain. This hypothesis was staunchly defended by Jacques Lafaye, who maintained that the testimony in its defense from 1531 to 1648 was "very weak" when compared to "the clear and convincing arguments" of the opposition. Therefore, he classified the apparition as a "Mexican myth," the product of popular fantasy. According to Lafaye, the "Guadalupan myth" was part of the movement that was necessary for the formation of a national conscience. In his opinion, one could find the origin of the myth in the book by Sánchez. For Lafaye, both the book by Sánchez (1648) and the one by Lasso de Vega (1649) would have had a great reception in Mexico and would have paved the way toward the recognition of Guadalupe as a national symbol of Mexico.

Finally, we recall Edmundo O'Gorman, according to whom, many wanted to see in the words of Montúfar what was not there, namely an implicit or indirect affirmation concerning the veracity of the apparitions and the supernatural origin of the image. O'Gorman also rejects the thesis of Garibay, who maintained that in the sermon by Archbishop Montúfar there was "an indirect affirmation of something extraordinary." For that reason, he concludes, no validity should be granted to *Información por el sermón de 1556* in the public process, since it had only a private character.

A third, intermediate, position can be found in more recent studies, such as those by Xavier Noguez (1993) and Richard Nebel (1995), and to me they seem to be the most acceptable. They do not deny the apparitions but affirm that, more than a typical historical documentation, there exists a continuous tradition, first oral and then written.

With the appearance of the book by Sánchez in 1648, the publication of the text by Lasso de la Vega in Nahuatl in 1649, and the diffusion of the tradition through the work of Luis Becerra Tanco (1666) and Francisco de Florencia (1688), the "official tradition" was firmly established concerning the events of Guadalupe.

The initial phase of the Guadalupe affair, characterized primarily by the creation of traditions originating out of oral and written testimony coming from local sources, was finished. According to Noguez, information regarding Guadalupe came out of Indian traditions that were interpreted in a Christian light. They did not come from documentation that was elaborated by the protagonists of either side.

Nebel is also of the opinion that there exists a tradition of the Guadalupan event, coming from either Indian or Spanish sources. Whichever opinion one wishes to accept about the historicity of the apparitions of Guadalupe, one thing is certain: with the tradition of the so-called event of Guadalupe, there arose a story to explain the event, and from the middle of the 17th century it was of extraordinary interest to people from every level of Mexican culture and society.

A new discovery

If, only a few years ago Noguez was able to affirm that "up until today no document from the official time of the apparitions has been found that can stand up to historical criticism and that could, therefore, be considered a proof of the historicity of the event" (X. Noguez, *Documentos guadalupanos*, 1993, p. 179), today a discovery has come to light that could be of fundamental importance for further research. It is a codex dated *"1548,"* discovered recently in a private collection, containing graphic elements and written dates that may prove of great interest. It was first announced officially in the magazine, *Maria y sus siervos*, 1995, 26, pp. 37-38, published by the Servites. The focal point of the work is an illustration of Juan Diego kneeling before Our Lady of Guadalupe, who stands in the clouds wearing a mantle studded with stars, while the sun peeps through the mountains at her back. The codex bears several inscriptions, including one which gives the date 1548 in the upper part above the mountains. Under the date one can read, in Nahuatl, "Also, in…1531… Cuauctlactoatzin… our beloved Mother Guadalupe appeared… Mexico." At the lower left one can see, under the sketch of Juan Diego, a writing which says: "he died a worthy death at Cuauctlactoatzin." There are also other writings that have not yet been deciphered.

The document refers to Blessed Juan Diego, called by his Aztec name, and to the fact of his death, which occurred around 1548, which possibly explains the reason for that date in the codex.

On the upper right there is a small sketch of Juan Diego, standing, and very similar to another sketch described by Father Mariano Cuevas in his *Album Histórico Guadalupano* as the most ancient picture of Juan Diego.

At the bottom on the right, beneath a pictograph attributed to Antonio Valeriano, there is a script which says: "*Juez anton vareliano*," which surely means: "Judge Antonio Valeriano." Also at the bottom, one can distinguish clearly the signature of Bernardino de Sahagún.

If this particular codex truly dates from the 16th century, as it seems to because of the signature of Sahagún, we have come to a very important point in the story of Guadalupe, one that precedes the book by Miguel Sánchez. In addition, it would confirm the Aztec name of Juan Diego, which began to be mentioned by Sigüenza y Góngora in the 18th century, without giving any reason for referring to him in this way.

Two other later illustrations also come from this codex. One of them was published in *La felicidad de México*, by Luis Becerra Tanco. Both illustrations, one original and the other a copy, are similar in style, but the one in "1548" seems more ancient, because of the lines and because of the material used. Nevertheless, they have much in common in regard to details; for example, there is a small and a large sketch of Juan Diego; the image of the Virgin of Guadalupe; the landscape, the vegetation and the sun. Father

Cuevas cites various experts who have verified that the etchings follow the conventional form typical of the 16th century, found also in the following century, but absent by 1700. And if this is true of the illustrations contained in *La felicidad de México*, then the *Codex* "*1548*," which is the original source, surely came first. Consequently, what can be said of the sketch in *La felicidad de México* can with equally good reason be said of the *Codex* "*1548*." In any case, it is necessary to continue the research to determine the origin and complete the information contained in the codex. It is not possible at present to make any definitive statement.

Conflicting opinions

When Luis Lasso de la Vega published his work in 1649, he stated that the *Nican Mopohua* and the *Nican Motecpana* were written by divine inspiration. This assertion has been refuted by the experts since the end of the 17th century. They maintain that Lasso had in his hands the original or a copy of the manuscript written in Nahuatl, since the account of the apparitions and the miracles by the Virgin of Guadalupe reveal a vision of the world of the Aztecs that Lasso could never have imitated. This is also the opinion of Luis Becerra Tanco, Carlos de Sigüenza y Góngora, Lorenzo Boturini Benaduci, José Ignacio Bartolache, Angel María Garibay and the majority of present-day Guadalupanistas.

It is known that Luis Lasso de la Vega published the text of *Nican Mopohua*, without a Spanish translation, in the first part of his work, but he did not indicate the sources used which would have served to clarify the question concerning the author and the destiny of the original document.

According to the new study by Nebel, cited above, among the various narrations of the Guadalupe tradition the *Nican Mopohua* is the most important because it has the reputation of uniting a belief with an historical event. In the *Nican Mopohua* there is a mixture of views of the European Christian world with those of the Aztec world. The Christian view is transmitted in Nahuatl, the most widely used language in New Spain. The form and content are interchanged, so that, as Nebel has said: "The Christian becomes a Mexican and the Mexican a Christian." Comparing the *Nican Mopohua* with other types of Mexican literature such as the *cantares* (popular poems and songs), Nebel has discovered surprising similarities which make it possible to conclude that the text is closely connected with other works written in Nahuatl.

Undoubtedly Luis Lasso de la Vega knew Nahuatl literature thoroughly. In his *Huey Tlamahuizoltica* he included a dedication, as was the custom in those times, so that his work would be appreciated as much as the works of other contemporary writers. Lasso de la Vega asserts that the traditions of his predecessors are insufficient for the purpose intended, namely, to offer an objective and orderly presentation, with no omissions, and to tell everything from the beginning. Consequently, he intends to present a complete work and at the same time to resolve for the first time the problem of the accounts of the apparitions and the miraculous impression of the image of Mary on the *tilma*. To do this in an orderly and objective manner is the only method worthy of faith in the Guadalupe event, and the only manner that will justify the veneration of the Virgin of Guadalupe by her Mexican children. For that reason the *Nican Mopohua* was conceived and developed to give a foundation for belief in the Guadalupe affair.

Already in the prologue Lasso de la Vega states that he has no literary ambitions but that he wants to be faithful to tradition. He was aware that the historians in his day placed more importance on the truth contained in the facts, that is, on the significance of the events narrated, than on their objectivity. For that reason, Lasso, or the author of the narrative of the apparitions, narrates the "facts" in conformity with the meaning he believes he discovers in the Guadalupan event. Endeavoring to place the event in an historical context, he bases the historical certitude on the certitude of faith. His intention is to unite indissolubly the Gospel to the events at Guadalupe and to develop them literarily and historically as a Mexican basis of Christian faith. The author narrates a truth that for him is existentially certain and it is important to transmit it to the colonial society. Consequently, the problem is not when and how the apparitions took place, but rather, what is the new world order entrusted to the inhabitants of New Spain? To what extent were they "subject to" the apparitions and what meaning do the apparitions have for the life of the Aztecs?

Nebel concludes by saying that in a certain way the *Nican Mopohua* contains the history of an incarnation. It deals with the history of the "social" birth of the Indians in New Spain. Thanks to the intervention of Guadalupe, the Indians are introduced to sociocultural relationships nourished by respect and at the same time they are brought into the realm of the history of Christianity, an ongoing process which is not yet over. The author does not declare himself in favor of the apparitions, but neither does he deny them, giving the event at Guadalupe a sociohistorical and cultural reading instead. The study by Nebel, done with seriousness and scientific objectivity, provides a significant contribution to the research both in its theological as well as in its sociological, historical and cultural context, even if it lacks a faith perspective.

Informaciones of 1666 and 1723

At this point it is necessary to provide some more details regarding the *Informaciones de 1666*, to which references have repeatedly been made. This work is considered to be fundamentally important both as a proof of the Guadalupe tradition and as a support to the life, virtues, reputation for holiness and cult of Blessed Juan Diego. This, in fact, was a conclusion in a recent study, namely, *Las informaciones jurídicas del 1666 y el beato indio Juan Diego* by A.M. Sada Lambretón (1991). It treats of the investigations carried out with all the juridical requirements of an ecclesiastical and civil tribunal in Mexico City in the years 1665 and 1666 in order to obtain from the Congregation of Rites [now known as the

Congregation for Divine Worship] permission for a Mass and proper Office for the celebration of the feast of Our Lady of Guadalupe. *Informaciones* presents a summary of this process requested by the Holy See during the pontificate of Pope Alexander VII and it documents the fact of the apparitions of the Virgin Mary of Guadalupe. It is a public, authentic and juridical document whose historicity is irrefutable and whose value is immense.

The first request for the cult was put forward by Canon Francisco Siles who in 1663 proposed the project to the bishop of Puebla and the Viceroy of New Spain, as well as to the chapter of the Cathedral of Mexico City. The initiative was favorably received. Siles proceeded to gather the authentic documents, and various letters were attached to the petition. Rome responded that in due time a "remissorial rescript" would be sent with the list of questions for examining the testimony, in order to clarify as perfectly as possible the facts surrounding the Guadalupan event.

At the end of 1665 nothing had yet arrived from Rome. Canon Siles felt that the response could be some time in coming and, fearing that the Indian witnesses at Cuauhtitlán might die due to their advanced age, he wanted to take some preparatory steps. He formally requested of the cathedral chapter that it begin a juridical process to obtain information and testimonial declarations concerning the apparitions. The ecclesiastical tribunal was established in December, 1665. The metropolitan chapter named the judges who were to conduct the interrogation of witnesses on nine questions concerning the fundamentally important points in the Guadalupan tradition, such as details about the identity of Juan Diego, the apparitions, the image of the Virgin on the *tilma*, the devotion which followed, the trustworthiness and good judgment of Juan Diego. After having answered the questions put to them, their depositions were read back and they were asked to ratify what had been set down. Between February and March of 1666, 135 years after the apparitions, depositions were taken from twelve Spaniards, ten ecclesiastics, and two lay persons. In April of the same year eight Indian witnesses were examined with the help of an interpreter. They were all from Cuauhtitlán, ranging in age from 90 to 115.

All of the depositions, made under oath, confirmed the oral and written traditions concerning the apparitions as well as the life of Juan Diego. The persons who provided the information testified on the words of people who had known Juan Diego and had heard from him or from his contemporaries the story of the apparitions. For example, the grandmother of the Indian Pablo Juárez had been present at the transfer of the image to the first little shrine ordered by the bishop.

The distance of 135 years is surely noteworthy, but it should be remembered that these witnesses had known directly persons who were alive at the time of the apparitions. Likewise, the witnesses, interrogated individually, testified that Juan Diego was regarded by all as a saint and presented as a model of Christian living who inspired others.

Luis Becerra Tanco took part in the *Informaciones* with a written declaration in which he stated that he had certain knowledge, gained from credible aged persons, that Juan Diego had passed the last years of his life as custodian of the primitive chapel and had died in the odor of sanctity. The text of the manuscript was published in the same year of 1666 under the title *Origen milagrosa del Santuario de Nuestra Señora de Guadalupe*.

The *Informaciones* reached the status of an apostolic process in 1894, the year in which was granted and approved the new Office of Our Lady of Guadalupe, in view of the pontifical crowning which was scheduled for October, 1895.

In fact, in 1721 the finding of copies of the documents from 1666 revived in the priest, José de Lizardi, treasurer of the sanctuary of Our Lady of Guadalupe, the desire to advance the petitions previously made. He passed to the bishop of Mexico City, José Pérez de Lanciego Aguilar, all the documentation, having noted that the Holy See had not given any reason to the contrary and had even given evidence of a desire to foster the devotion to Our Lady of Guadalupe. Lizardi received the support of the bishop, who commanded the diocesan ecclesiastical judge, Carlos Bermúdez de Castro, to inaugurate a new process. A commissary and several experts were named who could examine the image: two doctors and three painters. The interrogation was more detailed than the one in 1666 and it covered eighteen questions. The first person called to testify in May, 1723, was an individual of exceptional religious character, the Franciscan Fray Antonio Margil de Jesús, 66 years of age and a tireless missionary preacher, well qualified to testify to the expansion of the cult of Guadalupe. In June of 1723 the second witness gave testimony; he was dean of the metropolitan church of Mexico City, age 65, and he asserted that the persons questioned in 1666 were all worthy of belief. Then the process was interrupted again. Finally, in 1754, Pope Benedict XIV, through the Congregation of Rites, approved the Office and the proper Mass with the brief *Non est quidem* and confirmed the patronage of Our Lady of Guadalupe over New Spain and set the feast for December 12.

The *Informaciones* of 1666 and 1723, coming from persons of various backgrounds and social classes, constitute testimony that cannot be ignored.

Other writings from the 17th century

The writings and sermons of the clergy in the 17th century, especially those of the Jesuits, were very important in making Guadalupe the prophecy of a "new order." The year 1648 saw the publication of a work, *Imagen de la Virgen María Madre de Dios de Guadalupe* by Miguel Sánchez (1606?-1677). It was an emotional narrative, filled with beautiful metaphors, which probably fascinated the Indians, creoles and *mestizos* who were certain that they had a Mother in Our Lady of Guadalupe. In that book the conquest of New Spain was justified because it made it possible for the Virgin Mary to manifest herself in the land chosen by her and to establish in Mexico a new paradise. Just as Israel was chosen to receive Jesus Christ, so also Mexico was chosen to receive the Virgin Mary of Guadalupe, who will lead her children to the promised land. In this context, later authors saw colonial Mexico as the desert of Sinai and independent Mexico as the land of milk and honey.

The intention of the author was to show that the image of Our Lady of Guadalupe was a fulfillment of the prophecy in chapter 12 of Revelation. The interpretation by Sánchez gives a Mariological and ecclesial meaning to the biblical passage. Mary is the woman who appears in the heavens as a great sign, making evident the characteristics of the Church as Mother of believers. From this Marian and ecclesiological perspective Sánchez explains the prophetic character of chapter 12 of Revelation in relation to the Guadalupan event and the history of Mexico. In his mind this prophecy is realized by Mexico under two aspects: on the one hand, the vision of the pregnant woman who appears in the heavens, clothed in the sun and with the moon beneath her feet and a crown of twelve stars on her head is indeed a prophetic promise pointing to Our Lady of Guadalupe, who appeared to Juan Diego on Tepeyac and left her image impressed on his *tilma*. She appeared to Juan Diego as to a second John the Evangelist and to Bishop Juan de Zumárraga, a third John.

In another passage the woman dressed in the sun, who with her son is pursued by the dragon who is conquered in turn by St. Michael (or Hernán Cortés) and cast down to the earth, is a prophecy of the history of the Mexican people which was tainted with the idolatry of the Indian culture and saved by the intervention of the "evangelizing conquest" by the Spaniards. Once the demons of idolatry have been driven out, the Church flourishes in a new people in New Spain.

With this methodological process, Sánchez, in addition to showing the prophetic value of the biblical text, intended to create a biblical and theological basis for the image and the history of the apparitions. He was convinced that the apparitions of the Virgin Mary on Tepeyac and the image that appeared on the *tilma* of

Juan Diego should be considered historical facts. The authenticity of the apparitions and the image are for him a sign that "this miraculous Lady and creole saint" is Mexican and in its complexity, the history of Mexico is foretold in the Bible.

Luis Becerra Tanco (1603-1672) is considered "the third evangelist of Guadalupe," following Miguel Sánchez and Lasso de la Vega. He was a man of great culture and an expert theologian, and since he lacked authentic documents that could verify the apparitions of the Virgin Mary at Tepeyac, he felt that it was his duty to write what he knew about the tradition: what he had read in his youth in the writings of Indians and what he remembered from his early years. He wanted to convert the tradition into history. He wanted to show what is true and thus give a scientific foundation to the Guadalupan tradition "for the glory of the country, to which her sons should be dedicated," presenting the truth as it is. He did not want to take refuge in anecdotes nor appeal to theology, but to work as a man of science. According to Luis Becerra Tanco, a scientific analysis of the details would make it possible to demonstrate the veracity of the Guadalupan apparitions without any contradiction and without allowing room for equivocation. In this sense, the author, referring to what had been written in 1666, states: "This is the tradition in its entirety, simply and without any embellishment. It is so certain that were anything to be added to it, it would be, if not false, at least apocryphal."

Francisco de Florencia (1620?-1695), Jesuit professor of philosophy and theology, is the author of the "fourth Guadalupan gospel" with his book: *La Estrella del Norte de México, aparecida al rayar el día de la luz evangélica en este nuevo mundo.* In this book he puts his linguistic ability, his humanistic formation, and his theology at the service of the Guadalupan devotion in order to contribute something to its catechetical and pastoral dimensions. His intention is evident in his theological argumentation, which is useful for understanding the significance of the Guadalupan affair, and in his use of poetry and rhetoric, which help to stimulate the devotion of the reader. Florencia is addressing those who are educated in the faith and he presents material from dogmatic and moral theology, from his own biblical knowledge, from the history of the Church and from his connection with the event of Guadalupe and its significance for the Church and for theology in Mexico. At the same time, however, he addresses the ordinary people because they feel disenfranchised in piety and devotion and also in their *sensus fidei*. In the Prologue, he says that he feels obligated to complete the story of Guadalupe which has been handed down to us in tradition "out of love for the holy image" and "out of love for the Mexican nation." The book begins with a long digression on the legend of the founding of the city of Mexico-Tenochtitlán, the region in which the apparitions of the Blessed Virgin took place. From the dark night of idolatry arises the light of faith in the New World, thanks to the apparitions of Our Lady of Guadalupe. Consequently, for Florencia the Christianization of Mexico is based on the action of God and not on the act of conquest by Spain. Florencia, and not Benedict XIV, was the first to apply the passage of Scripture to Mexico: "He has not done thus for any other nation" (Ps 147:20). It is a slogan that should be the guiding theme of the Guadalupans and the fundamental truth behind the event in Guadalupe, to wit: "The Virgin Mary has not granted a similar privilege to any other people."

Convinced of the continuity of the tradition, Florencia recognized a definitive historical value in the *Informaciones de 1666*, from which he drew the details for his biography of Juan Diego, presented as an exemplary Christian figure.

According to Florencia, the image and the numerous favors shown to Mexico, as well as the devotion of the Spaniards, creoles and *mestizos*, are proof of the grandeur of Mexico, which is unique in the world by reason of the apparitions of Guadalupe. The publication of the works of Sánchez, Lasso de la Vega, Becerra Tanco and Florencia, known as the "four Guadalupan evangelists," marked the beginning of the popular enthusiasm that conferred grandeur and value to that which is Mexican and promoted the union of the various social classes. At the beginning of the 17th century, the apparitions were presented as an event of national significance. A large number of documents and monuments of various kinds were attached to the Guadalupan event and used it as a base. In the 19th century the war of independence incarnated the promise of the Book of Revelation, that the writers of the 17th and 18th centuries had applied to the events of Guadalupe: the promise of life offered by the heavenly Mother is transformed into the promise of Mexican independence. After a timid beginning in the 16th century, Guadalupanism reaches its peak in the 17th and 18th centuries; and it is preserved down to the present day.

Today the sanctuary of Our Lady of Guadalupe is perhaps the most frequented Marian shrine in the world; there are twenty million pilgrims each year. There are numerous manifestations of the devotion of the faithful by way of gifts, vows and prayer. Naturally, the most privileged celebrations take place on December 12, a day that is equivalent to Mother's Day, observed by all the children of Mary. The floral displays on that day are marvelous to behold. Numerous Indian groups improvise beautiful folk dances in honor of their Mother. There are also representations of pre-colonial times, before the coming of the Spaniards. Another manifestation of Marian devotion is the penitential aspect; for example, the last approaches to the basilica are made on their knees by countless pilgrims. Although some of the devotions might be considered exaggerations, one cannot deny the presence of a profound faith, especially among the simple people. As regards the prayers, they are usually the traditional ones, and especially the rosary, whether said privately or recited or sung solemnly by groups.

It is undeniable that the cult of Our Lady of Guadalupe is the center of popular Mexican religiosity. In their pastoral letter in 1978 the Mexican bishops recognized that the apparition of the Virgin Mary on Tepeyac has been a primary vehicle of the Christian faith, a model of popular religiosity and of proven evangelical value in the culture of the nation.

Conclusion

W E HAVE REVIEWED the salient phases of an event that has left a profound mark on Mexican culture and religiosity: the Queen of heaven appears to a poor Indian, speaking the same language. She does not use signs or gestures that could arouse fear and terror, but manifests her tender and delicate spirit by using cultural symbols that were proper to the Aztec world. Thus, she manifests herself as a kind and attentive Mother.

Her appearance marks the beginning of a new era. She is the unique Mother of God and a wise evangelizer who seeks the unity of her children and loves all humanity in Christ. She gives us the Author of life. If by his incarnation Christ embraces the totality of humanity, Our Lady of Guadalupe embraces a divided people and unites them into one believing Church, the People of God.

The process of the cultural and racial fusion from which the *mestizo* people are derived would have been slow and painful had it not been for the fact that in the heavens of the Aztecs there appeared a new sun which would never set again. Hope began to grow in the hearts of the people, nourished by the word that for centuries was infusing comfort and courage into multitudes of believers throughout the world who had passed through the same trials. In the words of Isaiah 62:4: "No more shall men call you 'Forsaken' or your land 'Desolate,' but you shall be called 'My Delight,' and your land 'Espoused.' For the Lord delights in you, and makes your land his spouse."

Among the new *mestizo* people who were setting out on the pathway of faith we can begin to see how Christianity became such a significant factor in their lives, for the Spaniards as well as for the Indians. God mysteriously disposes the Guadalupe event as a confirmation of the essential methodology of the Christian proclamation and the effective impulse of the same in those dramatic beginnings. This proves that Christianity is a phenomenon capable of dialogue with everything human, to the point that there does not exist anything else capable of undergoing such a transformation and of being embraced by persons in such diverse situations. The Guadalupe event helps to generate in Latin America the encounter between the indigenous Indian world and Christianity, albeit through a necessary purification.

What is the significance of the Guadalupe event today, especially for the pastoral work of evangelization? We are brought face to face with a Christological message: Our Lady of Guadalupe wants to help the children of this world find unity of faith in the same Father through the luminous example of his Son. It is Jesus that the Virgin wants to make known; He is the one she wants to be adored and praised in the shrine. So Mary opens the way to Jesus; to Him, the font of hope and unity, she wants to lead her scattered children.

To consider today the meaning of Guadalupe is to place oneself in the school of Mary, mistress of humanity and of faith, servant of the Word which is meant to shine forth in all its splendor, like the celestial image on the *tilma* of Juan Diego. To be receptive to the evangelizing work of Mary means to increase one's Marian devotion and to transform it into an inspiring motive for evangelization. An authentic Marian devotion will imitate the faith and availability of Mary and it will animate the practice of all the Christian virtues. Therefore it is not a question of neglecting the traditional practices, but of purifying them of every limitation or deviation.

The Guadalupan message reminds the people that they must be united with the Church to be able to walk together toward union with Christ, who does not hide from the people the need for conversion and authenticity. For this reason it is important that the people be instructed more deeply concerning their Christian obligations, avoiding the excessive commitment to external practices that do not represent a real change of mentality in the way they live their Christian faith. In fact, popular religiosity, in spite of the values which it brings, does not necessarily lead to a personal adhesion to Christ, dead and risen.

Christians have a great responsibility to penetrate society with the Gospel message. To do so they should look to Our Lady of Guadalupe, the model of inculturated evangelization and the proclaimer of a new vision of life which is engrafted on to that to which one is invited to make a commitment. Symbolically, she transforms the arid hill at Tepeyac into a paradise.

It is a question of giving witness to the true God and only Lord in such a manner that we find in Him the way, the truth and the life. It calls for the ability to know through faith how to distinguish between the criteria of Jesus and purely human criteria and seek the proper response to our new problems. In a word, we seek the power to overcome all difficulties and the inspiration to make Christian values an element of our progress.

> Through inculturation the Church makes the Gospel incarnate in different cultures and at the same time introduces peoples, together with their cultures, into her own community. She transmits to them her own values, at the same time taking the good elements that already exist in them and renewing them from within (Pope John Paul II, *Redemptoris missio*, n. 52).

Authentic evangelization has characteristics proper to itself. It bears the sign of a new reality, it opens hearts to experience joy, it increases hope, it answers the needs of every person, it leads to a response that transforms anyone who engages in it. No Gospel corresponds so perfectly to those characteristics as does the one preached by Mary in the way she lived her life.

Mary, in her fullness of grace, is the star that throws light on the Gospel; she is the one who evangelizes, the model of the evangelizing Church. And precisely because she is the immaculate one, by her sanctity she demonstrates the truth and efficacy of the word in her life. And she teaches us how to believe, to embrace, to respond humbly, generously and fully to that word in our own lives as well.

Appendices

ONE

Early Accounts of the Apparitions

INI N HUEY TLAMAHUIZOLTZIN
"This is the great marvel…"

by Juan González

T HIS IS THE GREAT MARVEL that our Lord God has worked through holy Mary ever Virgin. Behold her! Listen to the miraculous manner in which she expresses her desire to have a shrine built in her honor, which she would like to be called Saint Mary, Queen of Tepeyac.

It happened this way. A poor man of the people, a *macehual*, a true man of God, a man of the fields (a poor person, a poor *mecapal*) was crossing the summit of Tepeyac in search of some roots for food when he saw the beloved Mother of God, who called him and said to him: "My poor beloved son, go to the big city of Mexico and tell the bishop, the spiritual guide of the people, that I earnestly desire that here on Tepeyac a house should be built for me. A shrine should be erected here in which faithful Christians can pray to me. Here I shall be their advocate when they invoke me."

So the poor little man went to present himself to the bishop and said to him: "Excellency, I don't want to bother you, but the Lady from heaven sent me here. She told me to come to you and tell you her desire: she wants a shrine to be built in her honor on Tepeyac, where Christians can pray to her. She also said that she wants to show all her love there and she will come to the aid of all who invoke her."

But the bishop did not believe him, so he said to him at once: "What are you saying, my son? Perhaps you are dreaming or maybe you are drunk. If what you say is true, then tell the Lady that I have asked you for a sign so that we can believe what you say."

So our little man went back sad and the Queen appeared to him again. When he saw her, he said: "O my Lady, I went where you sent me, but the bishop did not believe me. He told me that perhaps I was either dreaming or I was drunk. He also told me that for him to believe, you should give me a sign to take to him."

Then the Queen, the beloved Mother of God, said to him: "Don't be sad, my son. Go and pick some flowers over there where they are growing."

It was only by a miracle that flowers were in bloom because in that season the earth was very dry.

When our man picked the flowers, he placed them in his *tilma*. Then he returned to Mexico City to tell the bishop: "Excellency, I bring you the flowers that the heavenly Lady gave me so that you would believe that what she desires is true and it is certain that she herself told it to me."

Then, when he opened his *tilma* to show the bishop the flowers, a miraculous image of the Queen was impressed on the cloth, so that the bishop finally believed. At the sight, all present fell to their knees and admired it.

Truly, it is only by a miracle that the image of the Queen was imprinted on the *tilma* of this poor man and today it is visible to all.

Those who are devoted to her come here to pray to her and she, with maternal affection, comes to their aid and grants them what they ask. Truly, if anyone recognizes her as their advocate and gives himself entirely to her, the beloved Mother of God immediately intercedes for him. Actually, to all who place themselves under her care, under her protection, she is most generous with her help.

HUEY TLAMAHUIZOLTICA

"She appeared marvelously…"

by Luis Lasso de la Vega

In 1649 Luis Lasso de la Vega knew the story of Guadalupe in Nahuatl. He gathered various documents to prevent their loss or destruction and he also added some material of his own. The title given to the collection is *Huey Tlamahuizoltica*, and it has five parts:

1. *Ilhuicac Tlatoca Cihuapille* ("O great Queen of Heaven"), the prologue composed by Luis Lasso de la Vega.
2. *Nican Mopohua* ("Herein is related…"), the story of the apparitions written by the Indian, Antonio Valeriano between 1548 and 1555 (English translation follows as no. 3).
3. *In Tilmatzintli* ("The Tilma"), a description of the image on the *tilma* of Juan Diego, written most likely by the same Antonio Valeriano (English translation follows as no. 4).
4. *Nican Motecpana* ("Herein are treated…"), story of the first miracles worked by Our Lady of Guadalupe and a brief biography of Juan Diego, written by Fernando de Alva Ixtlilxóchitl (English translation follows as no. 5).
5. *Nican Tlantica* ("This concludes…"), conclusion by Luis Lasso de la Vega, containing also an ancient prayer to the Virgin Mary.

NICAN MOPOHUA
"Herein is related…"

by Antonio Valeriano

*Herein is related in orderly fashion how the holy Virgin Mary,
Mother of God and our Queen, miraculously appeared recently on
the hill Tepeyac, which was thereafter given the name Guadalupe.*

At first she appeared to an Indian named Juan Diego; then she
appeared in the miraculous image to Fray Juan Zumárraga, shortly
after he was named bishop.

Ten years after the conquest of Mexico City, war came to an
end and there was peace in every village; the faith, like flowers,
began to bud and to blossom in the knowledge of the true God,
the author of life, and to establish its first roots.

During that time—the year was 1531—in the early days of
December, a poor man of the people, whose name according to
tradition was Juan Diego, a native of Cuauhtitlán but for the things
of God dependent on Tlatelolco, very early in the morning—it was
a Saturday—was going to Tlatelolco for prayer and the catechism
lesson.

When he reached the base of the hill called Tepeyac, dawn
was just breaking. Suddenly he heard beautiful music coming from
the hill, like the sound of a flock of rare birds, and when their voices
were silent, it seemed as if the hill resounded with the echo of their
song. Their music, extremely sweet and pleasing, surpassed that of
the *coyoltótotl* and *tzinitzcán* and that of all the other songbirds.

Juan Diego stopped to look and he thought to himself: "Am I worthy and deserving of what I am hearing? Am I dreaming or am I just waking up? Where am I? Maybe I have been transported to the place described by our ancestors, our grandparents: a land of flowers, corn, meat and every good thing. Am I perhaps in the earthly paradise?" Meanwhile he was looking toward the crown of the hill, the direction where the sun rises, which was also the source of the heavenly music.

First apparition

The music suddenly ceased and there was complete silence. Then, from the summit of the hill he heard a sweet voice call him by name: "Juanito! Juan Dieguito!"

Without hesitation he ventured forward toward the place from which the voice came. He did not feel any anxiety or any reason to fear. On the contrary, he felt happy and his heart was full of joy. So he began to climb the hill to see who it was that was calling him. When he reached the summit, he saw a young lady standing there, and she invited him to come closer.

When he stood in front of her, he was greatly moved by her charming appearance which was beyond all imagination. Her garments were radiant like the sun, as if reflecting its rays, and the stone on which she was standing was giving off rays of light; its splendor seemed like that of an anklet adorned with precious stones; the ground around her glistened like the rays of a rainbow in a dense fog. The *mezquites* and the *nopales* and other bushes that usually grow there were as brilliant as emeralds; the foliage seemed like turquoise; the branches, thorns and needles were shining like gold.

He knelt in her presence and listened to her words, which were very gentle and extremely affable, charming and pleasant. She said to him: "Listen, Juanito, my poor beloved son; where are you going?"

He answered: "My dear Lady and Queen, I want to go to your

little house in Mexico-Tlatelolco to take religious instruction which is given by our priests, the living witnesses of our Lord."

After this brief exchange, the Lady immediately revealed her precious will. "Know, my poor beloved son," she said, "that I am the ever Virgin and Holy Mary, the Mother of the one true God, of Him who is the author of life, the creator of men, of Him in whom all things subsist, of the Lord of heaven and Master of the earth. I strongly desire that in this place a little holy house should be constructed for me, that there be erected a shrine here in which I want to manifest Him, make Him known, give Him to all people through my love, my compassion, my help, and my protection, because I truly am your merciful Mother, your Mother and the Mother of all who dwell in this land and of all those who love me, invoke me, seek me and place all their trust in me.

"Here I shall listen to your weeping and lamentation. I shall take them all to my heart and I shall cure your many sufferings, afflictions and sorrows, bringing a remedy for them all. So that my merciful loving desires may be realized, go to the residence of the bishop of Mexico City and tell him that I am sending you to inform him of my wishes, namely, that he provide me with a house, that he build a chapel at the foot of this hill. You will tell him everything that you have seen and admired and all that you have heard.

"Be assured that I shall be most grateful to you and shall reward you; for doing this I shall enrich and glorify you. Your fatigue and the service that you perform for me in carrying out my request will be worthily compensated. Now that you have heard my words, my poor beloved son, go and carry out your mission."

Juan Diego bowed down before her and said: "My Lady, I go at once to carry out your word, to fulfill your wishes, and so for now this poor Indian leaves you." Then he hurriedly descended the hill and started out on the road which leads directly to Mexico City.

On entering the city, he went straight to the residence of the bishop, who only a short time before had been assigned to that country. His name was Fray Juan de Zumárraga and he was a

Franciscan. Arriving at the episcopal residence, Juan Diego asked the servants to tell the bishop that he would like to see him immediately. After a long wait the bishop sent word for him to enter, so they came to call him.

On entering, he bowed and knelt before the bishop. Then he began to report everything, repeating the precious words of the Queen of heaven. He reported everything he had admired, seen and heard. The bishop let him talk and listened to the message, but he did not put much faith in it. He dismissed him with the words: "My son, return again and I shall listen to you at greater leisure. I shall reflect well on the reason for which you have come and what you have told me."

Second apparition

Juan Diego departed, feeling sad because the task for which he had been sent was not immediately complied with. The same day he returned immediately and headed straight for the top of the hill at Tepeyac. Here he had the pleasant surprise of seeing that the Queen of heaven was waiting for him at the very place where she had appeared to him the first time.

As soon as he saw her he prostrated himself, throwing himself to the ground before her, and he said: "My Lady and Queen, my poor beloved daughter, I have been where you sent me to carry out your lovely mission. With great difficulty, I succeeded in meeting the bishop and I communicated to him the message you entrusted to me. He received me kindly and he listened to everything attentively, but I noticed that when he replied he did not put any faith in my words. He told me: 'Return again and I shall listen to you at greater leisure. I shall reflect well on the reason for which you have come and what you have told me.' From what he said, I perceived that he thinks that the request to build a chapel in this place does not come from you, but is the fruit of my own imagination. Therefore I ask you, my beloved Lady and Queen, to give the task of carrying your message to a person of some importance, who

is esteemed, known, respected and honored. Truly, I am a man of
the fields, a *mecapal*, a *cacaxtli*, a nobody.... I am a follower, a servant; I myself need to be led, to be carried on another's back. The
place where you sent me, my Virgin, my poor little Girl, is not
suitable for me; it is strange to me. Please excuse me. I also know
that in asking you this, I cause you some displeasure and vexation,
my beloved Lady, and I deserve your anger."

The holy Virgin, worthy of all praise and veneration, replied:
"Listen, my poor beloved son. They are not few, the faithful servants of mine, to whom I could entrust the task of carrying my
message. But it is very important that it should be you who goes
and no one else, and that through your mediation my desire be
realized and my will be brought to completion. Therefore, I earnestly beg you, my little beloved son, indeed, I command you to
present yourself again tomorrow to the bishop. Make him understand again what I want, so that he will construct the chapel that
I request; and tell him that it is I personally, the ever-Virgin and
holy Mary, the Mother of God, who sends you."

For his part, Juan Diego replied: "My beloved Lady and
Queen, I do not want to make you sad or grieve your heart. Will-
ingly I shall set out to fulfill your command; I do not want in any
way to excuse myself from doing it nor do I want to let myself be
frightened by the difficulty of the journey. I shall carry out your
will promptly, but perhaps they will not listen to me; and if they
do, probably they will not believe me. Tomorrow evening at sun-
set I shall return to tell you what the bishop says to me. For now, I
respectfully take my leave of you, my poor beloved Daughter.
Meanwhile, you must rest a while." He then returned quickly to
his house and went to sleep.

The following day was Sunday. Early in the morning, while
it was still dark, he left the house and directed his steps toward
Tlatelolco for the catechism lesson. Afterward he would go to see
the bishop. Around ten o'clock he was ready; he had attended Mass
and religious instruction; he had answered the roll call and the
people had all dispersed.

Juan Diego made his way to the bishop's residence. Arriving there, he insisted on being able to see the bishop, and after some considerable delay he was admitted. He knelt at the bishop's feet and burst into tears. Sobbing, he repeated again the message from the Queen of heaven, pleading with the bishop to believe his words which expressed the will of the Virgin and begging him to build the chapel in the place indicated.

To verify the credibility of what he had heard, the bishop asked many questions of Juan Diego, inquiring especially about the place where he had seen the Lady and what she was like. Juan Diego described everything to the bishop in great detail. Responding promptly to all the questions, he also said that evidently it was the Virgin Mary, the loving and marvelous Mother of our Lord Jesus Christ.

Not even this time did the bishop put faith in his words. He said that Juan Diego did not realize how much he was asking for, and only on the basis of his words. In order to believe that it was truly a message from the Queen of heaven in person, it was indispensable to have a definite sign.

After listening to the bishop, Juan Diego replied: "Lord bishop, tell me what kind of sign you are requesting, so I can ask the Lady from heaven who sent me." But seeing that Juan Diego had confirmed everything he had said previously and did not hesitate or doubt in the slightest, the bishop dismissed him without answering.

Then, as soon as Juan Diego had left, the bishop commanded a few of his trustworthy servants to follow him and see where he went, whom he saw, and with whom he spoke.

And so it was done. Juan Diego went directly to the road that leads out of the city. Those who were following him, however, lost sight of him on the wooden bridge that crosses the gorge near Tepeyac. Though they looked everywhere, they could find no trace of him, so they returned home. They were annoyed, not only because he had slipped out of sight, but because they had not been able to fulfill their mission.

They presented themselves to the bishop and tried to convince him not to let himself be deceived. They said that Juan Diego was surely lying, and that he was either a visionary or a dreamer. They concluded by saying that if Juan Diego should ever return, they would catch him and punish him severely so that he would not come back again to lie and make fools of them.

Third apparition

In the meantime, Juan Diego was with the holy Virgin, telling her the answer he had received from the bishop. After hearing this, the Lady said to him: "Very well, my son. Return here tomorrow and you can take to the bishop the sign he has requested. Then he will believe you. He will no longer doubt you or be suspicious of you. And know, my son, that I shall reward your solicitude, effort and fatigue on my behalf. Go now, and tomorrow I shall await you here."

But the following day, Monday, when Juan Diego was supposed to receive the sign to take to the bishop in order to be believed, he failed to return. In fact, he had no sooner arrived home than he found his uncle, Juan Bernardino, gravely ill. He hastily went to call a doctor, who provided some relief, but it was too late, for his uncle's condition was very serious.

During the night his uncle asked Juan Diego to return to Tlatelolco at the crack of dawn to get a priest to hear his confession and prepare him for a good death. He was certain that he was at the end of his life and would not recover.

Fourth apparition

On Tuesday, while it was still dark, Juan Diego took to the road and hurriedly headed for Tlatelolco to get a priest. Arriving at the footpath that borders Tepeyac toward the west, the route that he usually took when he went to the city, he thought to himself: "If I keep going on this path I shall probably meet the Lady again, who will detain me so that I can take the sign to the bishop as prearranged. For the moment, though, I must resolve the problem at hand. First of all, I must hurry and get the priest because my uncle is anxiously awaiting him."

So Juan Diego made a detour along the other side of the hill, to the east, in order to reach Tlatelolco quickly without being detained by the Queen of heaven. He thought that by taking this path he would not be seen by her, but she could see perfectly in all directions. As a matter of fact, when he began to go round the other side of the hill, she spotted him. She had been watching him. She approached him on the side of the hill, blocking his way, and said to him: "What has happened, my poor beloved son? Where are you going?"

Juan Diego felt bewildered and even ashamed; he was frightened and somewhat timid. He bowed before her and greeted her, saying: "My most beloved Lady, I hope all goes well with you. How are you this morning? Did you sleep well? I am going to cause you some displeasure. I want to tell you, my Lady, that one of your devoted servants, my uncle, is gravely ill. He has been struck with a serious sickness and will surely die. I am going in great haste to your house in Tlatelolco to call one of the beloved of our Lord, one of our priests, to come to his bedside to hear his confession and prepare him for a good death. Truly, we were born for this and we all await the difficult moment of our death. But as soon as I have finished this task, I shall immediately return here again, my Lady, to carry your message. I beg you to pardon me. Have yet a little more patience with me, my beloved little Daughter, because in acting this way I am not trying to deceive you. Tomorrow I shall come here in all haste."

After listening to the excuses of Juan Diego, the Most Holy Virgin responded: "Listen, my son, and take what I say to heart. Do not be afraid or troubled. Do not let your heart be disturbed and do not be worried about this or any other sickness. Am I not here, who am your Mother? Are you not under my protection? Am

I not the source of your joy? Are you not in the fold of my mantle, in the cradle of my arms? What more do you want? Nothing should afflict you or disturb you. Do not let the sickness of your uncle worry you; he will not die now. Know for certain that he is already perfectly cured." (At that very moment, as his uncle will later testify, he was cured immediately.)

When Juan Diego heard the loving words of the Queen of heaven, he felt greatly relieved and consoled. He then begged her to send him immediately to take to the bishop the sign that would cause him to believe in the message.

The heavenly Lady then asked him to go to the summit of the hill, where she had previously appeared. She said: "Go up, my beloved son, to the crown of the hill where you saw me and where I gave you a mission. There you will find a great variety of flowers. Cut them and arrange them into bunches. Then come back and bring them to me."

Juan Diego went up the hill immediately and when he reached the top, he was amazed at the great quantity of beautiful, freshly blooming Castilian roses, although it was out of season; in fact, it was the middle of winter. The flowers gave off a sweet aroma; they looked like precious pearls sprinkled by the dew of night. Juan Diego began to cut the flowers, arrange them in bunches and place them in his *tilma*. There is no question that the hilltop was not a suitable place for flowers to grow; it was full of stones, thistles, thorns, cactus and *mezquites*; and if perchance it were possible for plants to grow, this was certainly not the season. It was the month of December, the season when frost was common that destroyed all vegetation.

Juan Diego hurried back down the hill and carried the assorted flowers to the heavenly Lady. When she saw them, she took them into her venerable hands and rearranged them in his *tilma*, saying: "My poor beloved son, these different kinds of flowers are the proof, the sign that you are to take to the bishop. In my name tell him that these are the proof that my message is the expression of my will, which he should carry out. They are also the proof that

you are my messenger and that you are worthy of the greatest trust.
I strictly command you to open your *tilma* only in the presence of
the bishop; you will show to him alone what you are carrying. You
will tell him everything precisely. You will tell him that I commanded you to go to the top of the hill to cut flowers and you will
report to him everything that you have seen and admired. All this
is so that you may convince the bishop and he will decide to build
the chapel that I have requested, in conformity with my will."

As soon as the Lady finished speaking, Juan Diego started out
on the road to Mexico City. He went on his way very content. He
proceeded with a heart full of joy because he was certain that this
time everything would work out well and everything would be
brought to conclusion perfectly. He was very careful with what he
was carrying in the fold of his mantle so that nothing would fall
out and he delighted in the fragrance of the various precious
flowers.

When he reached the residence of the bishop, the secretary
and the other servants met him. He asked them to bring him to
the bishop, but no one paid him any attention. They pretended
not to hear him; perhaps it was still too early or maybe they remembered him from the last time and considered him an annoy-
ance. The servants who had previously followed him had reported
how they mysteriously lost sight of him. He would now have to
wait a long time before getting any response.

Although much time had already passed, he still continued
to stand there, with bowed head, not doing anything, just waiting
to be called. The servants, aware that he was carrying something
in his *tilma*, approached him to see what it was and to satisfy their
curiosity. When Juan Diego realized that there was no way he could
hide from them what he was carrying, and fearing that he might
crush or spill them, he opened the *tilma* slightly and showed them
that they were flowers. The servants saw that he was carrying precious, exotic flowers which were in full bloom, and they were amazed
at their freshness, their beauty and their aroma. Three times they
tried to snatch some of the flowers but it was impossible to pull any

of them out. In fact, each time they tried, the flowers drew back; it was as if they were embroidered or painted or sewn on the *tilma*.

They then hastened to tell the bishop about what they had seen. They told him that the Indian, who had been there before and this time had been waiting for a long time to be received, wanted to see him. Hearing this, the bishop realized that this could be the sign to convince him to do what the little man was asking, so he immediately gave orders to admit him.

On entering, Juan Diego knelt before the bishop as he had done before. Once again he repeated all that he had seen and heard and admired. He said: "Your Excellency, I have done all that you commanded. I went to the heavenly Lady, my Patroness, holy Mary, the beloved Mother of God, and I told her that you are asking for a sign in order to believe me and to proceed with the construction of her little house at the place she indicated. And I also told her, as you commissioned me to do, that I have given you my word that I would ask for a concrete sign of her will. She has kindly acceded to your desire and request so that her beloved will can be respected and carried out.

"And so today, very early in the morning, she has again sent me to you. Since she had promised to give me the sign that I had requested of her, she immediately fulfilled my request. She sent me to the top of the hill, where I had seen her previously, in order to pick a variety of Castilian roses. I have cut them and have brought them to you. She took them in her holy hands and arranged them in my *tilma*, so that I could bring them to you and turn them over to you alone. I knew that the top of the hill was not a suitable place for growing flowers, since it is full of stones, thorns, thistles, cactus, *mezquites* and *huizaches*, but I did not hesitate for a moment. When I arrived at the crown of the hill, I was able to admire a panorama of paradise. There was a great quantity of various kinds of flowers, bright and sparkling with dew. I picked the flowers and she told me to bring them to you in her name. This is the proof, the sign that you requested in order to carry out her loving will. This should also make clear the truth of my message. Here are the flowers. Be kind enough to accept them."

The image of the Virgin

Juan Diego then opened his mantle in which the flowers were deposited and no sooner had they fallen to the ground than on the *tilma*, in the sight of all, appeared the image of the ever-virgin holy Mary, Mother of God, in the form and figure that we see today preserved in her beloved house in the shrine at the foot of Tepeyac, which we invoke with the name "Guadalupe."

On seeing this, the bishop and all who were present fell to their knees, amazed and overwhelmed. They then rose to their feet to examine the image more closely and their faces were clouded with sorrow. They looked at the image, not out of curiosity, but with sincere hearts. With tears in his eyes and with mournful face, the bishop prayed and asked pardon for not being devout enough to accept her message and to carry out her will. Approaching Juan Diego, he removed the *tilma* on which the image of the Lady from heaven was impressed and immediately placed it in his chapel.

Juan Diego remained for a day in the residence of the bishop and was treated as a guest. On the following day the bishop said to him: "Let us go to see the place where the heavenly Queen wishes a chapel to be built." He then began immediately to look for people to build it.

After pointing out the place where the Queen of heaven desired the chapel to be constructed, Juan Diego asked permission to be excused. He wanted to return home to see his uncle Juan Bernardino, who was seriously ill when Juan Diego had left him to call a priest in Tlatelolco so he could go to confession and prepare himself for death. The heavenly Lady had already assured him that his uncle was fully recovered. But they did not let Juan Diego go home alone; some wanted to accompany him.

Arriving home, Juan Diego found his uncle perfectly cured and in good health. He was amazed to see that his nephew had returned in the company of so many people, and he asked what was the reason for this honor.

Then Juan Diego explained that when he left home to call for a priest, the Lady from heaven appeared to him at Tepeyac. She sent him to the bishop in Mexico City, to ask him to build a chapel at Tepeyac. She had also told him not to be worried about the health of his uncle, because he was cured. This gave him a great deal of comfort.

Fifth apparition

Juan Bernardino confirmed that the Lady from heaven had cured him at that precise moment. He also stated that he had seen her in exactly the same form as she had appeared to his nephew. He added that he also had been given the task to go to the bishop in Mexico City and as soon as he would have the opportunity to see him, he should report to him everything that he had seen and the miraculous way in which he was cured. Last of all, he said that the Lady from heaven had told him the title by which the sacred image should be venerated: *The Perfect Virgin, Holy Mary of Guadalupe*.

Then they escorted Juan Bernardino to see the bishop so that he could bring him up to date concerning everything that had happened and could give his testimony. The two of them, uncle and nephew, remained guests of the bishop for several days, until the little chapel was erected to the Queen of heaven on Tepeyac, on the spot where she had been seen by Juan Diego. The bishop, meanwhile, had the *tilma* with the image of the Lady from heaven transported to the principal church. He had it taken from his private chapel, so that all the people could admire and venerate it.

Everyone in the city, with no exception, came to gaze upon and pray before the holy image. They knew about its supernatural origin, and they presented their petitions in front of it. They were amazed at the miraculous manner in which it was imprinted on the *tilma* of Juan Diego; in fact, the image had not been painted by any human being on earth.

IN TILMATZINTLI
"The Tilma"

by Antonio Valeriano

The *tilma* on which the image of the Lady from heaven was miraculously imprinted was the *ayate* of Juan Diego, a coarse material but well sewn. The *ayate* was the garment worn by poor Indians; only nobles and the warriors wore garments made of cotton. The *tilma* worn by Juan Diego was made from *ichtli*, or threadlike strands from the *maguey* plant. The *tilma* on which the image of the Ever Virgin, our Queen, appeared was made of two pieces of cloth sewn together at one end with a fine thread and worn over the shoulders, with the two lengthy pieces hanging down the front and the back.

The height of the blessed image, from the feet to the little crown on her head measures four feet nine inches. Her beautiful face is serious and noble but somewhat dark. Her posture is humble and her hands are folded in front of her chest, at the height of her cincture. The cincture itself is violet in color. Only the right foot reveals the toe of the shoe, which is ash-colored. Her tunic, so far as it is visible, is pink, but in the shaded areas it is bright red or ruby. The pattern of the tunic is that of various flowers, all in bloom, outlined in gold. At her neck she wears a round, golden brooch with black lines surrounding it and a cross in the center. Another soft, white garment can also be seen underneath which encircles the wrists snugly and has a highly embroidered pattern. The outside of her mantle is sky-blue, and it flows down from the top of her head to her feet, without ever covering her face. The mantle is pulled back, as it were, to reveal the front of the tunic. Its border is relatively wide and is of gold, with approximately forty-six gold stars scattered throughout.

Her head is inclined to the right, and on top of her head, above the veil, is a crown of gold with spires tapering upwards that are wider at the base. The crescent moon is under her feet, with its points facing upward. Her image is in the center of the sun, which sends forth its rays from behind the Lady, surrounding her entirely. There are one hundred golden rays, some very long and others short, like flames. Twelve surround her face and head, and some fifty in all on either side. Around the periphery there is a white cloud which follows the outline of the whole.

This precious image moves supported by an angel, whose figure terminates at the waist and nothing is seen of its lower body. It is as if the angel is emerging from the cloud. The extremities of the mantle and clothing of the Lady, which reach all the way down to her feet, are held up by the hands of the angel, who is dressed in a red tunic with a gold collar. His outspread wings are covered with brightly-colored long feathers. The hands of the angel hold up and support the Virgin and he seems quite content to thus carry the Queen of heaven.

NICAN MOTECPANA
"Here are treated..."

by Fernando de Alva Ixtlilxóchitl

Here are treated in orderly fashion all the miracles performed by the Lady from heaven, our Blessed Mother of Guadalupe.

The first time that they carried the image of Our Lady of Guadalupe to Tepeyac, after the little chapel had been constructed, the first of all the miracles performed by her took place. There was a huge procession accompanied by all the ecclesiastics, no one was excluded. There were Spaniards under whose authority the city was, all the noble Mexicans and other persons who had come from various places. Everything along the road was decorated, from Mexico City to Tepeyac, where the chapel of the Lady from heaven was built. Everyone marched in the procession with great jubilation. The way was jammed with people, and on the lake, which was very deep, there were many canoes carrying natives, and some of them were making skirmishes on the lake. One of the archers, dressed according to Chichimeca custom, stretched his bow and inadvertently let the arrow fly. It struck one of the other natives in the throat. This is what happened. Seeing that he was already dead, they brought the victim to shore and laid his body in front of the image of the Virgin, our Queen, whom the friends and relatives invoked, asking that she would bring him back to life. After they extracted the arrow, not only did he regain life, but the wound was completely healed. The only things that remained were the marks where the arrow had entered and emerged. The man rose to his feet, and the Lady gave him the strength to walk, infusing him with great joy. All the people were moved at the sight and they praised the Immaculate Lady from heaven, Holy Mary of Guadalupe, who in this way fulfilled the promise made to Juan Diego always to help and defend the natives and all who call upon her. It is said that the poor Indian remained from that time on in the little chapel of the Lady from heaven, sweeping the yard, the chapel and the entrance.

In the year 1544 a plague came upon the city and many people died. Without any doubt there were a hundred persons buried each day. The city was gradually being depopulated. The Franciscan Fathers, seeing that there was no letup nor was there any known remedy, but the plague was advancing and extending to other areas, seeing that the Lord, the giver of life, was destroying the nation, suggested that there should be a procession and all should go to Tepeyac. So the Fathers gathered together many youngsters, both male and female, around the ages of six or seven. They all gathered together and formed a procession that set out from Tlatelolco. During the entire march the people invoked the Lord to take pity on his people and cease his anger and have compassion out of love for his precious Mother, our most pure Queen, the Holy Mary of Guadalupe of Tepeyac. At last they reached the chapel, where the friars led numerous, fervent prayers. And God, the author of life, willed that through the intercession and prayers of his compassionate and blessed Mother, the plague should end at once. On the very next day it was noticed that fewer people were buried; and in the end there were only two or three, until the plague ended completely.

From the beginning, a short time after the faith came to this land which is called New Spain, the Lady from heaven, the most pure Holy Mary, loved these natives very much and came to their aid so that they would give themselves to the true faith and reject idolatry in which they had lived in error and the dark night in which they were held as slaves by the devil. And in order that they would call upon her and place themselves in her hands, she appeared to two of them. The first, who merited to receive the image of our most pure Queen and is here, close to Mexico City, was Juan Diego at Tepeyac of Guadalupe. Then the image, which we call *"de los Remedios,"* appeared to Don Juan in Totoltépec. He saw it when he was among the *maguey* plants at the top of a small hill where her little chapel now stands. He took it to his home, where he kept it for some years and then, to preserve it, he put it in a little shrine in front of his house. The image had been there for some time when Juan was struck down with the plague. And realizing that he was seriously ill and could not care for himself or even rise from his bed, he asked his sons to carry him to Tepeyac which is several miles from Totoltépec, to our most precious and pure Mother of Guadalupe. He knew that the Lady from heaven had cured Juan Bernardino, the uncle of Juan Diego, originally from Cuauhtitlán, who had also contracted the plague. So his sons immediately arranged for a wooden litter and carried him to Tepeyac.

After they placed him before the Lady from heaven, our blessed Mother of Guadalupe, he prayed to her with tears and asked her to do him the favor of curing him so that he could remain some time longer on earth to serve her and her beloved Son. She listened to his prayer with benevolence; it pleased her greatly to hear his petition and she smiled as she looked at him. When she spoke, it was with much love: "Arise, because you are cured, and return to your home. I command you that, where you saw my image at the top of the hill where the *maguey* grows, you should build a chapel to contain it." She also commanded some other things. He was cured instantly. Then, after praying some more and giving thanks for the great benefit received, he returned home on his own feet. They no longer had to carry him on a litter. Once he got home, he immediately set his hands to the task of building the little chapel to contain the precious image of the Lady from heaven which is called *"de los Remedios."* When the chapel was completed, she herself entered and placed herself on the altar, as she is found to-day and as she is seen in all her miracles.

A Spanish nobleman of Mexico City, named Antonio Carbajal, traveled to Tollantzinco with a young relative. Passing through Tepeyac, he stopped for a few moments at the little chapel of our most pure and precious Mother of Guadalupe. There, they hastily saluted the Queen of heaven and asked her to help them and protect them so that they would reach their destination safely. After they had left and were on their way, they were discussing the events of Guadalupe: how the image of the Virgin had appeared and how many miracles had been worked for those who had in-voked her help. While they were traveling, the horse on which the young relative was riding fell down, either because he was sud-denly frightened or he had made a misstep. Then quick as a flash the horse leaped up and began to run swiftly through the crags and ravines. The rider tried in vain to bring the horse to a stop, pull-ing with all his strength on the reins, but to no avail. This went on for several miles, while his companions were at a loss to know what to do.

His companions finally lost sight of the youth and they ex-pected they would find him broken and mangled because the di-rection in which his horse was racing was very dangerous, full of crevices and stones. But our Lord and his precious and merciful Mother wanted to save him. When his companions found him, the horse was standing still, with his head lowered and his legs bent; he could move no further. The young man was hanging by one foot, which was caught in the saddle. On seeing this, his companions were amazed that they found him alive and apparently unhurt.

They took him in their arms and freed his foot from the stirrup When he was on his feet, they asked him how he was saved from harm, since he had no cuts or bruises. He replied: "You have already seen that on leaving Mexico City, we paused for a short time at the house of the Lady from heaven, our precious Mother of Guadalupe, and we admired her blessed image and prayed to her. Then, as we proceeded, we were discussing the miracles she had performed and how her image had appeared miraculously. I remembered it all very well. Consequently, when I found myself in the midst of great danger and was in no way able to help myself, and in any case I was going to be lost or die and I was beyond all help, then with all my heart I called upon the most pure Lady from heaven, our precious Mother of Guadalupe, to have pity on me and help me. Then all at once I saw her, just as she appears in our precious image of our Mother of Guadalupe; she had come to my aid and saved me. She took the reins of the horse and he halted at once, he obeyed her and bowed before her, just as you found him when you arrived." They all fervently praised the Lady from heaven and then they proceeded on their journey.

On another occasion a Spaniard was praying on his knees before the Lady from heaven, our precious Mother of Guadalupe. And it happened that the cord from which a very heavy lamp was suspended, broke and fell right on his head. Everyone in the chapel thought that he surely must have been killed and his skull fractured, or that he must have been seriously injured, because the lamp fell from a great height. But as it turned out, no injury was suffered; and not only that, but the lamp was perfectly intact. The glass on the lamp was not broken, the oil was not spilled, and the flame was still burning. All the people were in admiration of the miracle performed by the Lady from heaven.

Juan Vásquez de Acuña had the image under his care, being vicar for many years. It once happened that when he was about to celebrate Mass at the main altar, all the candles went out. The sacristan tried to light them, but he delayed a little. While the priest waited for the candles to be lit, he saw two flames come out from the rays of sunlight on the image, which relit the candles on each side. Many persons in the church marveled at this miracle.

A short time after the Lady had appeared to Juan Diego and her image was miraculously imprinted on his *tilma,* she performed numerous miracles. It is said that in that very spot behind the chapel of the Lady, to the east, at the spot where she descended to appear to Juan Diego, a fountain of water burst forth. Juan Diego on that occasion had not wanted to be seen by the Lady from heaven because he was on his way to call a priest to hear the confession of his uncle, Juan Bernardino, to prepare him for death because he was seriously ill. It was the same spot that she had pointed out to him and commanded him to gather flowers at the top of the hill. It is also the place where she told him the chapel should be built, and from that same spot she sent him to the bishop to have him build the chapel. The water which came forth there from the fountain did so very gently and not with force. The water itself was clear, with a strong odor and not pleasing to the taste. It was in fact a bit on the acid side but good for all kinds of infirmities for those who agreed to drink it or bathe in it. Numerous were the miracles which the Lady from heaven, our precious Mother, Holy Mary of Guadalupe, worked with that water.

A Spanish woman living in Mexico City began to suffer from a swelling in her stomach, as from dropsy, and it seemed as if eventually she would burst. The Spanish doctors tried all sorts of medication and therapy but nothing did any good or alleviated her condition; rather, her stomach kept swelling more and more. She was afflicted in this way for ten months and felt sure that she would die if the Lady from heaven, the most pure Mary of Guadalupe did not cure her. So she asked to be transported on a litter to Tepeyac, to the chapel of the Lady from heaven. Rising early in the morning, they carried her to the little chapel and placed the stretcher in front of the image. The woman prayed earnestly, asking the Lady to have pity on her and to restore her to health. She asked the attendants to give her a little water from the fountain, and when she drank some of it, she became calm and fell asleep. At noontime the lady was still sleeping, so the people who had brought her to the chapel decided to step outside and let the sick woman rest. One of the natives who was sweeping the chapel in compliance with a personal vow he had taken, saw that from beneath the sick woman emerged a terrifying snake, as long as an arm and quite thick. Terrified, he called out to the Spanish woman, who woke up at once and shrieked with fear, calling out for help. The snake was killed and the woman was immediately cured and her stomach was deflated. She stayed there for four more days, praying to the Lady from heaven who had graciously cured her. When the woman returned home, it was not necessary for her friends to carry her on a litter, but she walked on her own two feet, quite happy at not suffering any bad consequences.

A Spanish nobleman, resident of Mexico City, was suffering from a severe headache and pain in the ears. Nothing could relieve the pain and he reached a point where he could not stand it any more. He asked to be taken to the little chapel of the Virgin, our precious Mother of Guadalupe. When he arrived at the chapel, he poured out his heart in supplication, asking that she cure him, and he made a vow to offer her the sculpture of a head carved out of silver as a votive offering. He had scarcely arrived at the chapel when he was cured. He remained for nine days in the house of the Lady. He then returned home completely cured and no longer suffered pain.

A young girl named Catalina suffered from dropsy. Seeing that nothing did her any good, and when her condition became worse, the doctors told her that she must not even attempt to rise from her bed, for fear of dying. Then the girl asked to be taken to the chapel of the Lady from heaven, our precious Mother of Guadalupe. Arriving at the chapel, she prayed with all her heart to be brought back to health. Then, with great confidence, she drank some of the water from the fountain and was immediately cured. Scarcely had she drunk the water, when the air came out of her body, and especially the mouth. By that time it was evening and she was no longer suffering any pain, thanks to the visit to the chapel of the Lady.

A discalced Franciscan brother, Fray Pedro de Valderrama, had a very serious infection in one of his toes. Nothing was of any avail and it seemed as if it would have to be amputated. He was taken to the chapel of Our Lady of Guadalupe and on arriving, they loosened the bandage on his foot and showed the infected toe to the Lady from heaven, praying earnestly that she would heal it. Their prayer was answered immediately and the friar was able to return on his own feet to the friary at Pachuca.

A Spanish nobleman named Luis de Castilla, also had a foot that was badly swollen and inflamed. He was in a very bad condition because the leg was putrid and the doctors now no longer tried to apply any medication in hope of a cure. He was certain that he was going to die. It is said that the Franciscan friar mentioned above, told him that he had been cured by the Lady from heaven, our precious Mother of Guadalupe. So the man ordered a foot carved out of silver, the same size as his own, and sent it to the chapel to be hung in front of her image. And he prayed with all his heart for the Virgin to cure him. When the messenger was sent to deliver the silver foot to the chapel, the sick man's condition was so serious that he wanted to die; but when the messenger returned, he found the man in good health. The Lady from heaven had cured him.

A sacristan named Juan Pavón who was in charge of the chapel of the Lady from heaven, our beloved Mother of Guadalupe, had a son who was suffering from a serious infection in his neck and was in grave condition. He wanted to die, because he could get no relief anywhere. They took him to the chapel of the Lady and anointed his neck with oil from the lamp that was burning there. In an instant the Lady from heaven cured him.

Whenever the precious image of our dear Mother of Guadalupe was displayed, all the citizens around here asked her to protect them and come to their assistance in their needs. And at the hour of their death they placed themselves entirely in her hands. Among these was Francisco Quetzalmamalitzín, a gentleman from Teotihuacán, when the village was destroyed and left without any defense, because all the people were opposed to the departure of the Franciscan friars. The Viceroy, Luis de Velasco, wanted to be placed in charge of the friars at St. Augustine, but the citizens considered this to be a great imposition. Meanwhile, Don Francisco and his followers could no longer hide anyplace; they were being sought everywhere. So he came at last to Azcapotzalco and prayed in secret to the Lady of Guadalupe to inspire the Viceroy and the gentlemen of the Royal Audience (Tribunal) to grant pardon to the inhabitants of the village so they could return to their homes and the Franciscan friars could also return. That is precisely what happened: all the citizens were pardoned and allowed to return to their homes and the Franciscan friars were permitted to return to St. Augustine's. This incident occurred in 1558. And then, at the hour of his death, Don Francisco commended himself to the Lady from heaven, our precious Mother of Guadalupe, that she look with favor on his soul. He made a bequest in her honor, as is evident in the first lines of his last will and testament, which was notarized on March 2, 1563.

Innumerable are the miracles that have been worked by the most pure and heavenly Lady of Guadalupe, since she is in her chapel for the benefit of both the natives and the Spaniards. In a word, all the people have invoked her aid and followed her. Juan Diego was completely dedicated to his patroness and was unhappy that his home and village would be too far away for him to serve her daily and sweep the chapel, so he asked the bishop to let him stay in some place closer to her chapel, in order to serve her. The bishop acceded to his request and provided him with a small house next to the chapel of the Lady from heaven. In fact, the bishop loved him very much. So Juan Diego immediately left his village and moved into the little house; he left to his uncle Juan Bernardino his house and land. Each day he occupied himself with spiritual things and cleaning the chapel. He prostrated himself before the Lady from heaven and invoked her with devotion. He went to confession and Communion often; he fasted, performed penances and took the discipline; he wore a penitential belt and concealed himself in the dark in order to pray in solitude and call upon the Lady from heaven. He was a widower. His wife, whose name was María Lucía had died two years before the first apparition of the Immaculate. The two of them had lived chaste lives and they had both remained virgins. He had never known a woman. In fact, on one occasion he listened to the preaching of Fray Toribio Motolinía, one of the original twelve Franciscan friars. The friar said that chastity was very pleasing to God and his Blessed Mother; that all things are granted to one who prays to the Blessed Mother; and finally, the chaste who recommend themselves to her care, will be granted whatever they desire, whatever they request, as well as release from their afflictions.

His uncle, Juan Bernardino, seeing that Juan Diego served our Lord and his Blessed Mother very well, desired to follow him and be with him, but Juan Diego did not want that. He told his uncle that he would do much better to stay in his own house in order to take care of the house and lands which their fathers and grandfathers had left to them, because the Lady from heaven had disposed matters so that only Juan Diego should remain at the little chapel. In 1544 Juan Bernardino was struck down by the plague. When he was in serious condition, he saw the Lady from heaven in a dream and she told him that it was his time to die but that he should be comforted and not be disturbed, because she would protect him and she would conduct him to his heavenly abode, since he had always been dedicated to her and had always prayed to her. He died on May 15, 1544, and his body was taken to Tepeyac to be buried in the chapel of the Lady from heaven. All this was done under the authority of the bishop. At his death, Juan Bernardino was 86 years old.

After serving the Queen of heaven for sixteen years, Juan Diego died in the year 1548, at almost the same time as the bishop. At the time of his passing, the Lady from heaven appeared to him and told him it was time to leave to enjoy in heaven what she had promised him. Juan Diego was also buried in the chapel. He was 74 years old when he died. The Blessed Lady and her beloved Son took his soul to the joy of heavenly glory.

We can also serve her in this way and she will liberate us from all the deceptive things of this world so that we can enjoy eternal bliss in heaven. Amen.

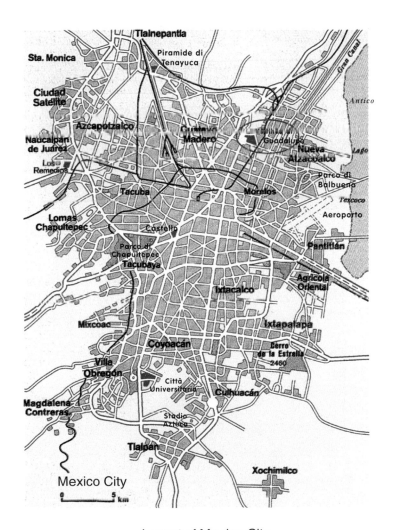

Layout of Mexico City

The complete image of Our Lady of Guadalupe measures 195 x 105 cm. (approx. 6.3' x 3.5'). The cloth, on which it remains miraculously imprinted, was the mantle (called a *tilma* or *ayate*) of Juan Diego. The *tilma*, worn by the Indians for warmth or to help them carry heavy weights, was made up of two pieces sewn together by a fine thread. Through the centuries, the *tilma* of Juan Diego has undergone some modifications in order to fit it into the various frames in which from time to time it was displayed.

A detail of the face and hands. The face resembles that of a young woman of mixed race. In fact, it is known as the *Morenita* (dark-skinned woman). The hands are the most compromised part of the picture in that they have been notably modified. Originally they were 12 mm. (0.4") longer.

Codex "1548" (on leather, 20 x 13.3 cm. or approx. 8" x 5"). This is the most ancient historical document testifying to the reality of the facts and persons relative to the events of December 1531. Recently discovered, it has been the object of various studies — appearing in the Appendix of the *Enciclopedia Guadalupana* (Mexico City, 1997) — that have determined its date and authenticity.

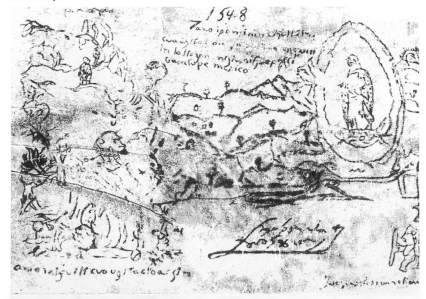

In the presence of the bishop, Juan Diego opens his mantle containing the flowers that he had gathered at the command of the Madonna on Tepeyac. Imprinted on the open mantle the figure of the Virgin appears miraculously. The scene, painted by Manuel Cabrera toward the middle of the 1700's, is extraordinarily similar to that reflected in the eyes of the image, discovered by means of electronic instruments at the beginning of the 1980's.

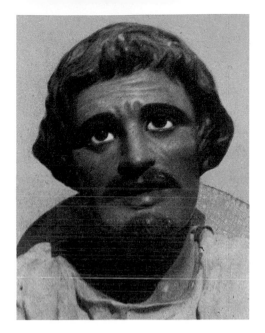

Juan Diego, the visionary of Tepeyac, in a modern likeness carved out of wood. His Aztec name was Cuauhtlotatzin ("he who speaks like an eagle"). He was baptized in 1524 and in December of 1531 received the apparitions of the Madonna. He died in 1548.

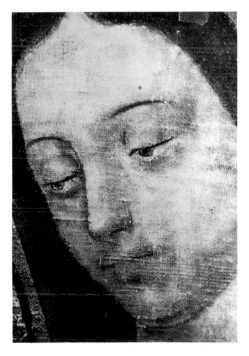

The face of the Virgin of Guadalupe in an infrared photo. The use of this technique allowed for fairly precise information regarding the pigments used and the eventual retouches the image has undergone.

This design makes plain the essential elements present on the *tilma*. The position of the stars has been studied in a special way by Mario Rojas Sánchez. Here we see the principal constellations which he was able to identify on the mantle of the Virgin.

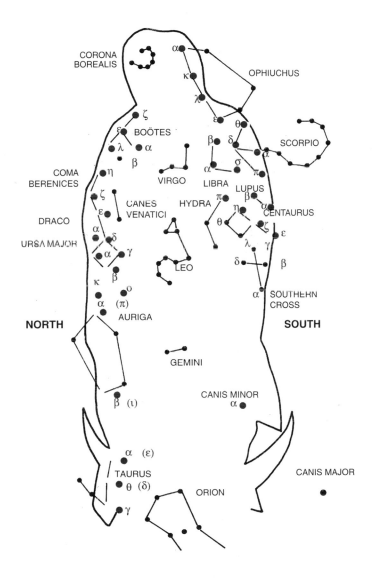

Mario Rojas Sánchez discovered a correlation between the stars on the mantle of the Virgin and those of the sky during the winter solstice in 1531. Here we can see reconstructed the constellations and principal stars. The stars present on the mantle of Our Lady of Guadalupe are shown in red. Notice how some of the constellations, while not being represented explicitly, fall into significant positions: the Corona Borealis on the forehead; Virgo on the joined hands; Leo on the swollen belly; Orion, the mythical giant, on the angel upholding the Virgin.

The new basilica of Our Lady of Guadalupe. Designed by four Mexican architects it was solemnly inaugurated on October 12, 1976 with the transfer of the image from the old to the new basilica. All the Mexican bishops and an enormous crowd of pilgrims were present.

Inside the new basilica on the occasion of the papal visit of Pope John Paul II on January 27, 1979. The pope returned on May 6, 1990 for the beatification of the visionary Juan Diego and again in January 1999. The new basilica can accommodate up to 12,000 and there is space for another 30,000 on the plaza outside.

Two

Codex "1548"

We previously mentioned the interesting discovery of *Codex "1548"* in a private collection. At some distance from the time of its drafting, we are now able to summarize the results of the study of the document by experts.

In the appendix to the four volumes of the work *Enciclopedia Guadalupana* (1997) one can find the results of the work that permit us to determine the time in which the *Codex "1548"* was written and its authenticity.

It should be noted that we are dealing here with a rectangular document, 20 by 13.3 cm., written on natural-colored tanned animal skin which was covered with yellow varnish and had become wrinkled due to the passage of time. The lines are traced in sepia and black. In addition to the date, 1548, there are two sketches of the apparitions of Our Lady of Guadalupe: the fourth apparition, at the foot of the hill, which is larger, and the first, at the top of the hill, in which one can fairly clearly see the figure of Juan Diego, while the profile of the Virgin is more obscure. Also evident are the pictograph of Antonio Valeriano and the signature of Fray Bernardino de Sahagún. There are also various inscriptions in Nahuatl with Latin letters, according to the style of the Indian students at the College of Santa Cruz in Tlatelolco, taught most likely by Sahagún.

In May, 1995, a commission was formed to coordinate the studies destined to prove scientifically the authenticity of the Co-

dex. Among the members were Mario Rojas Sánchez, a chemical engineer and historian who is at the same time an expert in the Nahuatl language, and Father Xavier Escalada, the publisher of the *Enciclopedia Guadalupana.* Some experts in the study of ancient manuscripts indicated that the principal lines of research should be into the signature of Bernardino de Sahagún, the material on which it was written, the ink and the subject matter of the manuscript.

As regards the signature of the eminent Franciscan, it was studied by Dr. Charles E. Dibble, professor at the University of Utah in Salt Lake City. He has dedicated a great part of his life to the investigation of the works by Sahagún and possesses the most complete collection of his signatures from various dates. In a letter of June 12, 1996, Dr. Dibble concluded that the signature that appears on the *Codex "1548"* is that of Fray Bernardino Sahagún because of certain typical characteristics: the three crosses, the manner of writing the word "fray," and the letters "d" and "b." Dr. Dibble concluded that the probable date of the signature must be placed between 1550 and 1560.

If we turn to the experts at the Office of Documentation and Photography at the Bank of Mexico, whose conclusion is dated September 18, 1996, we find that "the signature in question, attributed to Fray Bernardino de Sahagún, which appears in *Codex "1548,"* is from his hand and is therefore authentic." The agreement among the experts marks the conclusion of the research into the signature of Sahagún.

To verify the date of the *Codex,* we turn to the Institute of Physics at the National Autonomous University of Mexico City, which presented the conclusions of its research on January 30, 1996. The commission agreed not to submit the *Codex* to any tests that could possibly damage it in any way.

The two sides of the skin were examined under the microscope, and it was seen that the tracings were absorbed by the skin, except at the points where the lines were very thick, and ink smudges formed. As to the coloring, it was noted that where there is a concentration of ink, the lines are black with points of blue, and in lines that have a lower concentration of ink, the color is sepia with tones of yellow in some parts and bright red in others. The date 1548 is distinguished by its finesse and has a reddish hue. The entire area of the document is covered with a yellow varnish, and for that reason it would be impossible to modify the designs, the letters, or the numbers without leaving a mark that would be discernible with the microscope. The conclusion is that *no part of the document has been altered*.

The document was photographed at the Institute of Physics at the National Autonomous University of Mexico City, using different kinds of film: color and black and white, normal and sensitive to infrared rays, with and without filters. Through color enlargement it was possible to discern in the date 1548, a hyphen between the numbers 4 and 8, and also a stain. The conclusion reached by Ana Catalina Izquierdo was: "The infrared photography reveals absolutely nothing that is not visible to the naked eye; this supports the opinion that we are not dealing with metallic pigmentation." This supposition was later confirmed at the Institute of Physics.

As regards the content of the *Codex,* in the central upper part there appears the number 154-8 (instead of 1548, not uncommon when Indians transcribed Arabic numerals) in a reddish color. Under the date there are four lines written in Nahuatl by a native in an irregular, scarcely legible calligraphy which, according to the translation by Rafael Tena, reads as follows: "In the year 1531 our beloved Mother, the Lady of Guadalupe in Mexico appeared to Cuauhtlactoatzin."

According to Carlos de Sigüenza y Góngora, Cuauhtlactoatzin was Juan Diego's name before he was baptized. The drawing at the left of the upper central section portrays an Indian on his knees and wearing the traditional *ayate* tied on the right shoulder. He is in profile, with his glance looking out to the right. There is also a figure of the Lady of Guadalupe in the midst of clouds but without the crown or rays of light or the angel. The sketch represents without doubt the final apparition of the Virgin to Juan Diego at the base of the hill of Tepeyac. At the upper right of the central section is a drawing of the sun, peeping over the mountain tops. On the opposite side there is a drawing of an Indian wearing the *ayate* and a sketch of the Lady, almost entirely obliterated.

On the right hand side of the document, under the sun, there is an unusual sketch which has not been identified in a satisfactory manner. It shows an Indian, seated and looking to the left, holding a baton in his hand. Above his head is the head of a bird and a torrent of water. Undoubtedly the sketch represents the pictograph of Antonio Valeriano. Under the sketch is written: "Juez anton vareliano." "Juez" is Spanish for judge. For the significance of the misspelling of Valeriano, see p. 122. The sketch is similar to another one in the *Codex Aubin*, *2ª Parte* (1573), except that the figure here is looking to the right instead of the left. In his *Estudios de escritura tradicional Azteca-Náhuatl*, Joaquín Galarza states that the pictograph for a Christian name is an attempt to reproduce phonetically the Spanish name. This would explain the illustration of the head of a bird and the torrent of water, because the name Antonio is broken down into two words: *atl*, meaning eagle, and *tototl*, meaning water. According to Becerra Tanco, the Aztecs used the symbol of the person in command during the years in which some event is illustrated or described, so that one would be able to place the dates for events in history. Now, we do not know the year in which Valeriano was born, but we do know that he died in 1605, as stated by Juan de Torquemada, who says in his work *Monarchia indiana* (1613; Book 5) that Valeriano was a professor at the College of Santa Cruz and was governor of (the Indians in) Mexico City for forty years.

In the *Codex Aubin*, which dates back to 1573, there is a reference to Judge Antonio Valeriano and an allusion to the fact that he was governor of Mexico City in 1570. Mariano Cuevas estimates that Antonio Valeriano was born in 1516, so he would have been thirty-two years old in 1548. Consequently, in view of the foregoing, Valeriano could have been a judge when the Codex "1548" was composed.

In the lower central portion of the document there is a signature that is attributed to Fray Bernardino de Sahagún. At the left, in Nahuatl the text reads: "*Omomoquili Cuauhtlactoatzin*," meaning that "Cuauhtlactoatzin died in high esteem."

One of the major challenges for the experts had to do with the type of ink that was used. The Institute of Physics suggested that an analysis be done using Particle-Induced X-Ray Emission. They obtained sixteen samples from various parts of the Codex and were able to verify that there was no resin or synthetic material by which the ink could be affected. The substances present in rather high degree are calcium, sulphur and chlorine. The lack of any traces of iron or aluminum indicates that *the inks used are of an organic, animal or vegetable origin*. All of this is in conformity with the results obtained with the infrared spectroscope. The conclusion of the Institute of Physics is categorical: "On the basis of preceding studies there are sufficient elements to affirm the authenticity of Codex "1548" as a document that was elaborated in the 16th century."

Now, once the experts determined that the document in general and the signature in particular are authentic, we are able to put faith in the date that appears on it, namely, 1548.

In the Appendix of the *Enciclopedia Guadalupana* there is also an attempt to reconstruct the history of the Codex "1548." The students of the College of Santa Cruz knew Juan Diego and even interviewed him in order to hear the account of the apparitions *viva voce*. One of them gathered it all together in an orderly text called *Nican Mopohua*. And probably, at the death of Juan Diego they thought to compose a document in his memory. It is possible that Antonio Valeriano participated in the writing, together with some of his former classmates. Then, when it was completed, it is likely that they asked Fray Bernardino de Sahagún to affix his signature.

The first person to inherit this document, together with nu-

merous others like the *Nican Mopohua*, was Fernando de Alva
Ixtlilxóchitl, who passed it on to Luis Becerra Tanco, who then
bequeathed it to his son Juan, who in turn gave it to Carlos de
Sigüenza y Góngora.

All of this can be deduced from the declaration of Becerra
Tanco, according to which Fernando de Alva gave him a document
in Nahuatl concerning the apparitions, which he translated. The
account was included in his posthumously published book entitled
La felicidad de México. Becerra Tanco specifies that their forefathers
preserved the memory of events by means of paintings on deerskin
or the skin of some other animal, tanned in such a way that it served
as parchment. In addition, it was customary to include the figure
of the one governing and other important persons during whose
reign the events were said to have taken place. Among the facts
represented, there were also the apparitions at Tepeyac. In particular
Becerra Tanco claims to have seen in the hands of Fernando de
Alva numerous maps and chronicles of events, among which was
the representation of the miraculous apparition of Our Lady of
Guadalupe and the sketch of Juan Diego on his knees. It seems
certain that he was describing the *Codex "1548."*

Nor should we forget that at the beginning of the posthumous
work *La felicidad de México* a print was published which is so similar to the *Codex "1548"* that it seems impossible to say that this
was a mere coincidence. The print, which belongs to Becerra
Tanco, was made from an engraved piece of wood or metal which
reproduced numerous copies. The original, however, was undoubtedly prior to 1675, the year of the publication of *La felicidad de
México*, and more precisely, goes back to approximately 1590. The
origin of the engraving was not Mexico but Spain: Juan Diego had
been sketched by someone who had never seen an Indian up close,
because the features are definitely Spanish. Also, the lake at the
base of the hills denotes that the author knew very little about the
geography of the place of the apparitions, although the cloth tied
at the shoulder is exactly the way the Indians used to tie the *ayate*.
At the foot of the page there is a legend that has characteristics

typical of the 16th century, such as the manner of writing "a" and "p" and the statement: "Nuestra Señora de Guadalupe aparece en México."

This reproduction, called the *Sevillana*, is not the only one that derives from the *Codex "1548."* There is another one by Antonio de Castro, inspired by the details of the one we are discussing and which the historian Mariano Cuevas defines as "the most ancient drawing of Juan Diego." Its value is that it gives evidence of some of the traits that are almost obliterated, such as the image of the Madonna in the first apparition on the hill, which is scarcely discernible on the *Codex*, and the figure of Juan Diego, which is much clearer. It is probable that Antonio de Castro had known the *Codex "1548"* through Becerra Tanco. When, in 1666, Becerra Tanco published *Origen milagroso del Santuario de Nuestra Señora de Guadalupe*, that is, the first version of *La felicidad de México*, he chose this Guadalupan image bearing the signature of Antonio de Castro.

As to the supposition that Sigüenza y Góngora had possessed a copy of the *Codex "1548,"* that is based on the fact that he preserved all the documents belonging to Fernando de Alva Ixtlilxóchitl and received by his son Juan de Alva. We should not forget that Sigüenza y Góngora is the only one who said with certainty that the Nahuatl name of Juan Diego was Cuauhtlactoatzin, without giving the source of that information.

With the discovery of *Codex "1548"* we are in possession of the only document prior to that of Sigüenza and the probable source of its information, given the fact that it twice mentions the name Cuauhtlactoatzin. What we have said thus far authorizes us to think that Carlos de Sigüenza y Góngora had the *Codex "1548"* in his hands.

Finally, in 1931 a modest little work under the title *México y la Guadalupana*, which had among its authors the Director of the National Archives, Francisco Fernández del Castillo and reproduced illustrations by "unpublished or little known authors," was published. In a footnote on page 25 there is a pictograph which seems to have been copied right out of the *Codex "1548."* It is a reference to Valeriano and it makes the same mistake, spelling his name as "Vareliano" instead of "Valeriano."

Finally, knowing that the codex in question carries the signature of Sahagún, who died in 1590, we can be certain that it is from the 16th century and that the illustrations and engravings deriving from it are said to have been published for the first time, the first three in the 17th century and the rest in the 20th century.

There are some who doubt the authenticity of the signature of Bernardino de Sahagún, since a year later this great missionary wrote in his *Historia general de las cosas de la Nueva España* that "nothing for certain" is known about the construction of a chapel dedicated to Our Lady of Guadalupe on the hill where formerly there had been a temple dedicated to the pagan goddess Tonantzín. We should not forget that Sahagún wrote his opinion of the apparitions while Francisco de Bustamante was Provincial of the Franciscans, and Bustamante had stated that the image on the *tilma* of Juan Diego had been painted by an Indian named Marcos. A good reason why anyone would have been prompted to say this is the fear that the Indians would fall back into idolatry. However, we are not justified in saying that Sahagún intended to deny the apparitions at Tepeyac.

The *Codex "1548,"* therefore, seems to repudiate the silence concerning the book by Miguel Sánchez, written in 1648, a fact that induced some to doubt the historicity of the apparitions. The conclusions presented in the Appendix of the *Enciclopedia Guadalupana* constitute a definitive judgment that permits us to affirm that we are now faced with a document contemporary with the time of the apparitions which passes the examination of critical historians and can be considered a proof of the historicity of the event.

December 12, 1997
Querétero, Mexico

Noteworthy Events

1168 — Nahua tribes arrive in the Anahua Valley.

1325 — The foundation of Mexico City (Tenochtitlán) is begun.

1469 — Marriage of Ferdinand II and Isabella. The union of the kingdoms of Aragon and Castile results in the formation of Spain.

1474 — Birth of Juan Diego Cuauhtlatoatzin.

1476 — Birth of Juan de Zumárraga.

1480 (?) — The birth of Montezuma (Moctezuma) II.

1492 — Christopher Columbus discovers America (the Island, "San Salvador"). On the perilous journey back to Spain, fearing shipwreck, Columbus invokes the protection of Our Lady and promises to visit the Shrine of Our Lady of Guadalupe in Estremadura, Spain, if she delivers him and his crew safely home. King Ferdinand and Queen Isabella also visit the Shrine.

1504 — Hernán Cortés arrives in the New World.

1505 — Montezuma II elected Emperor of the Aztecs. Their capital is Tenochtitlán (Mexico City).

1511 — Hernán Cortés assists Velazquez in the conquest of Cuba.

1519 — Feb. 2: The beginning of the year C-1 Acátl, the year of Quetzalcóatl.

1519 — Feb. 18: A group of Spaniards with 10 ships, 100 sailors, 508 soldiers, along with 16 horses and a great deal of artillery under the command of Cortés leave Havana, Cuba and sail toward Mexico.

1519 — Mar. 12: Cortés anchors off the coast of what is now Veracruz.

1519 — Mar. 25: Cortés wins the Battle of Tabasco.

1519 — Apr. 22: Good Friday. Cortés erects a cross at Veracruz and the first Mass is celebrated on Mexican soil.

1519 — Sep. 23: Cortés enters Tlaxcala.

1519 — Nov. 8: Cortés arrives at Tenochtitlán (Mexico City) and is received in peace by Montezuma II, who later recognizes Emperor Charles V of Spain as his king.

1519 — Nov. 14: Cortés places Montezuma under house arrest.

1520 — Jan 27: The year of C-1 Acátl ends and with it the power of Quetzalcóatl.

1520 — June 29: Montezuma is deposed and dies.

1520 — June 30: La Noche Triste ("The Night of Sorrow"). The Spanish are driven out of Tenochtitlán. Three-fifths of the Spanish perish in battle.

1520 — July 12: Cortés returns defeated to Tlaxcala where he is received as a friend.

1520 — August: A terrible epidemic of smallpox kills many Indians in Tenochtitlán.

1521 — May 12: Cortés lays siege to Tenochtitlán and after ninety-three days, on August 13, 1521 the Emperor Cuauhtémoc is captured.

1523 — August: Three Franciscan friars arrive in New Spain: Pedro de Gante, Juan Dekkers and Juan van den Auwera.

1524 — May 13: The twelve Franciscan "apostles," among them Motolinía (Toribio Paredes de Benevente), arrive on Mexican soil.

1525 — Motolinía was the priest who most probably baptized the Indian, Cuauhtlatoatzin, Juan Diego, his wife (who was given the name María Lucía), and his uncle Juan Bernardino.

1525 — Sept. 5: Cortés is expelled from the government of Mexico.

1525 — Oct. 11: Pope Clement VII creates the first Mexican Diocese and Charles V of Spain designates Tlaxcala as its cathedral seat.

1528 — The Franciscan friar, Juan de Zumárraga, arrives. Cortés is recalled to Spain. Juan Diego's wife, María Lucía, dies and Juan Diego moves to Tolpetlac to live with his uncle, Juan Bernardino.

1530 — Pope Clement VII creates a new diocese in Mexico City and Friar Juan de Zumárraga is appointed as its first bishop.

1531 — At the end of the year new Spanish officials are installed.

1531 — Dec. 9: Feast of the "Holy Conception of Mary" (defined by Pope Pius IX in 1854 as the Immaculate Conception). Early morning: first apparition of Our Lady of Guadalupe to

Juan Diego on Tepeyac Hill, once the site of the shrine of the Aztec mother-goddess Tonantzín.

1531 — Dec. 9: Afternoon: second apparition of Our Lady of Guadalupe.

1531 — Dec. 10: Third apparition of Our Lady of Guadalupe.

1531 — Dec. 12: Fourth apparition of Our Lady of Guadalupe. Image of Our Lady on Juan Diego's *tilma*.

Dec. 12: Fifth apparition of Our Lady of Guadalupe; to Juan Diego's uncle, Juan Bernardino, who is cured.

1531   Dec. 26: Translation of the image of Mary to the chapel and the first miracle at the foot of Tepeyac Hill. Juan Diego soon after moves into a little hut adjacent to the chapel where he lives for the remaining seventeen years of his life as custodian of the chapel and of the portrait.

1533 — Construction of a new and larger chapel or hermitage.

1535 — Don Antonio Valeriano, author of the *Nican Mopohua*, is one of the native founders of the Franciscan College of Santa Cruz de Tlatelolco.

1539 — In these seven years, eight to nine million Indians are converted according to Motolinía.

1540 — Antonio Valeriano writes the *Nican Mopohua*, the oldest written account of the apparitions.

1544 — The plague kills 12,000 in Mexico City but ends with the procession and prayers of little children (six and seven years old) to the shrine.

1544 — Juan Bernardino dies at the age of 84.

1548 — Death of Juan Diego at age 74.

1556 — The second Bishop of Mexico City, Alonso de Montúfar, OP, builds the church that became known as the Old Church of the Indians, thus indirectly showing his approval of the apparitions.

1568 — Bernal Díaz del Castillo, the renowned historian, refers in his writings to Guadalupe and its daily miracles.

1570 — Archbishop Montúfar, OP, sends to King Philip II of Spain a complete inventory of the archbishopric, including a mention of the little chapel of Our Lady of Guadalupe at Tepeyac and an oil painting of Our Lady which had been touched to the original. The King had it placed in the cabin of Admiral Giovanni Andrea Doria before the Battle of Lepanto.

1605 — Antonio Valeriano dies.

1629 — September 21: Beginning of the flood in Mexico City, resulting in the death of 30,000 Indians and 1,600 Spaniards. The holy image is transferred to the cathedral for safekeeping until it can be returned "on foot."

1634 — May 14: Our Lady's image is returned to Tepeyac in solemn procession.

1649 — Luis Lasso de la Vega, Vicar of Guadalupe, publishes his work in Nahuatl, *Huey Tlamahuizoltica*, which includes the *Nican Mopohua* of Antonio Valeriano.

1666 — Work is begun on a new chapel where Our Lady first appeared, and the juridical proceedings (*Informaciones Cánonicas Guadalupenas de 1666*) are held in which elderly Indians of Cuauhtitlan (Juan Diego's birthplace) report the story as they had received it from their elders, five of whom had heard it from Juan Diego himself.

1709 — Apr. 27: Dedication of the great new sanctuary of Our Lady of Guadalupe.

1723 — The plague strikes and lasts for eight months. Throughout Mexico a total of 700,000 persons die. Our Lady of Guadalupe is declared "Patroness of Mexico City" and shortly thereafter the plague ceases.

1737 — April 27: Our Lady of Guadalupe proclaimed the "Patroness of the whole of New Spain" (from California to El Salvador); the feast is celebrated on December 12 and is also a civil holiday.

1754 — April 24: The Congregation of Rites issues a decree approving the Office and Mass for Our Lady of Guadalupe. On May 25, Pope Benedict XIV, quoting the words of the 147th Psalm, "He has not dealt thus with any other nation," proclaims Our Lady of Guadalupe Patroness of Mexico.

1777 — June 1: The chapel of the well (*El Pocito*) is completed on the eastern side of the *Plaza de Mexico*.

1810 — Father Miguel Hidalgo carries the picture of Our Lady of Guadalupe as a standard proclaiming Mexican independence from Spain. War with Spain begins.

1821 — October 12: Agustín de Iturbide, first Mexican emperor after independence from Spain, puts the nation under the protection of Our Lady of Guadalupe.

1846 — Twenty-two bishops from the United States petition Rome to have the Virgin of Guadalupe declared Patroness of their country.

1887 — March 12: Pope Leo XIII orders the coronation of Our Lady of Guadalupe.

1894 — Pope Leo XIII approves a new Office and Mass for Our Lady of Guadalupe.

1895 — October 12: Coronation of Our Lady of Guadalupe by the Archbishop of Mexico and the personal delegate of Pope Leo XIII.

1904 — Aug. 24: The Shrine of the Virgin is raised to the status of a Basilica by Pope St. Pius X and Our Lady of Guadalupe is named Patroness of Latin America.

1921 — Nov. 14: During the Calles regime a bomb, concealed in a vase of roses, is placed under the image, destroying much of the altar, but miraculously not the Tilma. A cast-iron crucifix next to the Tilma is twisted out of shape, but even the protective glass covering the Tilma is not damaged.

1926 — Jesus García Gutiérres (1875-1958), a Mexican priest, restores the text of the Nican Mopohua from various fragments.

1933 — Dec. 10: Coronation of Our Lady of Guadalupe in Rome and repetition of the declaration that she is Patroness of Latin America.

1945 — Oct. 12: Pope Pius XII commemorates on the radio the golden anniversary of the crowning of the image of Our Lady, "Queen of Mexico" and "Empress of the Americas."

1966 — May 31: Pope Paul VI sends a Golden Rose to the Shrine of Our Lady of Guadalupe.

1970 — Oct. 12: Pope Paul VI makes a Telestar appearance to the people of Mexico to commemorate the 75th anniversary of the crowning of her image as "Our Lady Queen of Mexico" and "Empress of all the Americas."

1976 — Oct. 11: Dedication of the new basilica and transfer of Our Lady's image from the old to the new basilica.

1979 — Jan. 27: The first visit of Pope John Paul II to the Shrine where he proclaims the Virgin of Guadalupe the "Star of Evangelization," and "Mother of the Americas."

1990 — May 6: Pope John Paul II makes a pilgrimage to Mexico and, along with three Tlaxcalan boy martyrs and a Mexican priest, beatifies Juan Diego proclaiming December 9th, the date of the first apparition, as his feast.

1999 — The liturgical celebration of the Virgin of Guadalupe on December 12th is raised to the rank of a feast in all the countries of the Americas including all of the dioceses of the United States by the Congregation for Divine Worship and the Discipline of the Sacraments.

Bibliography

Sources

Ernesto de la Torre Villar - Ramiro Navarro de Anda, *Testimonios Históricos Guadalupanos*, Ed. Fondo de Cultura Económica, México, D.F., 1982.

— *El pregón de Atabal* (1531), p. 23.

— *Relación primitiva de las apariciones* (1541-1545) or *Inin Huey Tlamahuizoltzin*, pp. 24-25.

— Antonio Valeriano, *Nican Mopohua* (1552-1560), pp. 26-35.

— Fray Francisco de Bustamante, OFM and Fray Alonso de Montúfar, O.P., *Información por el sermón de 1556*, pp. 36-141.

— Bernal Díaz del Castillo, *Grandezas de Nueva España* (1550-1568), pp. 145-147.

— Martín Enríquez de Almanza, *Carta al rey Felippe II* (1575), pp. 148-149.

— Bernardino de Sahagún, *Sobre supersticiones* (1976), pp. 142-144.

— F. González de Eslava, *Canción a Nuestra Señora* (1577?), pp. 150-151.

— Miguel Sánchez, *Imagen de la Virgen María Madre de Dios de Guadalupe* (1648), pp. 152-281.

— Luis Lasso de la Vega, *Huey Tlamahuizoltica* (1649), pp. 282-308.

— Carlos Sigüenza y Góngora, *Primavera indiana* (1662), pp. 334-358.

— Fortino Hipólito Vera, *Informaciones sobre la milagrosa Aparición de la Santísima Virgen de Guadalupe, recibidas en 1666 y 1723*, Imprenta Católica, Amecameca (Estado de México, 1889), pp. 1338-1377.

— Luis Becerra Tanco, *Origen milagroso del Santuario de Nuestra Señora de Guadalupe* (1666; with a new title: *La Felicidad de México*, 1675), pp. 309-333.

129

— Francisco de Florencia, S.J., *La Estrella del Norte de México* (1688), pp. 359-399.

Monumenta Histórica Guadalupanensia: III. Documentario Guadalupano (1531- 1768), Centro de Estudios Guadalupanos, Ed. Tradición, México, D.F., 1980.

— *Anales de Juan Bautista* (indigenous document), p. 107.

— *Anales de Bartolache* (indigenous document), p. 109.

— *Anales de la catedral* (indigenous document), p. 111.

— *Códices Gómez de Orozco* (indigenous document), pp. 113-114.

— *Anales de Chilmalpain* (or *Chilmalpahin*) (indigenous document), p. 115.

English-language Studies

Carroll, Warren H., *Our Lady of Guadalupe and The Conquest of Darkness* (Front Royal, VA 22630: Christendom Publications, 1983).

Cawley, Martinus, *Guadalupe from the Aztec*: English translation of *Nican Mopohua* (P.O. Box 97, Lafayette, OR 97127: Guadalupe Translations, 1968).

———, *Anthology of Early Guadalupan Literature* (P.O. Box 97, Lafayette, OR 97127: Guadalupe Translations, 1968).

Feeney, Robert, *Mother of the Americas* (Leesburg, VA 22075: Aquinas Press, 1995).

Handbook on Guadalupe, A (P.O. Box 667, Valarie, NY 12184: Franciscan Friars of the Immaculate, 1996).

Johnston, Francis, *The Wonder of Guadalupe* (Rockford, IL 61105: Tan Books and Publishers, 1981).

Jones, Christine, *Prince of Eden: The Whole Story of Juan Diego* (P.O. Box 38, Blaine, WA 98231: Guadalupe Film Committee, 1999).

Leies, Herbert, *Mother for a New World, Our Lady of Guadalupe* (Westminster, MD 21157: Christian Classics).

O'Leary, Bede, *Our Lady of Guadalupe, Hope of America* (Lafayette, OR 97127: Trappist Abbey, 1974).

Rahm, Harold, *Am I Not Here?* (Washington, NJ 07882: Blue Army, 1979).

Rengers, Christopher, OFM Cap., *Mary of the Americas, Our Lady of Guadalupe* (Staten Island, NY 10314: ST PAULS / Alba House, 1990).

Royer, Franchón, *The Franciscans Came First* (Paterson, NJ: St. Anthony Guild Press, 1951).

Smith, Jody Brant, *The Image of Guadalupe, Myth or Miracle?* (New York, NY: Image Books, Doubleday & Co., 1984).

Foreign-language Studies
(relative to Our Lady of Guadalupe)

F.J. Clavijero, *Breve ragguaglio della prodigiosa e rinomata immagine della Madonna di Guadalupe di Città del Messico*, G. Biasini all'insegna di Pallade, Cesena, 1782.

F.H. Vera, *La milagrosa Aparición de Nuestra Señora de Guadalupe, comprobada por una información levantada en el siglo XVI*, Amecameca (Estado de México), 1890.

M. Cuevas, *Album histórico guadalupano del IV Centenario*, Ed. Salesiana, México, D.F., 1931.

P. Velásquez, *La Aparición de Santa Maria de Guadalupe*, Ed. Jus, México, D.F., 1931.

A. Pompa y Pompa, *Album del IV Centenario guadalupano*, Basílica de Guadalupe, México, D.F., 1938.

A.M. Garibay, *La maternidad espiritual de María en el mensaje guadalupano. Conferencias leídas en los Congresos Mariológicos de 7-12 de octubre de 1955 y 9-12 de octubre de 1960*, Ed. Jus, México, D.F., 1961.

L. López Beltrán, *La protohistoria guadalupana*, Ed. Jus, México, D.F., 1966.

L. López Beltrán, *Album del LXXV Aniversario de la Coronación Guadalupana*, Ed. Jus, México, D.F., 1973.

E. Hoornaert, *La evangelización según la tradición guadalupana*, in Equipo Pastoral, *María en la Pastoral popular*, Ed. Paulinas, Bogotá, 1976, pp. 89-111.

J. Lafaye, *Quetzalcóatl y Guadalupe. La formación de la conciencia nacional en México*, Ed. Fondo de Cultura Económica, México, D.F., 1977.

V. Elizondo, *Nostra Signora di Guadalupe simbolo di una cultura: "la forza dei deboli,"* in *Concilium*, 13 (1977), n. 2, pp. 35-48.

F. de J. Chauvet, *El culto guadalupano del Tepeyac*, Ed. Tradición, México, D.F., 1978.

Conferencia del Episcopado Mexicano, Exortación pastoral, *La presencia de Nuestra Señora de Guadalupe y el compromiso evangelizador de nuestra fe*, Ed. Paulinas, México, D.F., 1978.

Monumenta Historica Guadalupanensia: I, C.E.G., Ed. Tradición, México, D.F., 1978.

C.E.G., *Primer Encuentro Nacional Guadalupano, 7-8 septiembre de 1976*, Ed. Jus, México, D.F., 1978.

Monumenta Historica Guadalupanensia: II. *Juan Diego, el vidente del Tepeyac*, C.E.G., Ed. Tradición, México, D.F., 1979.

C.E.G., *Segundo Encuentro Nacional Guadalupano*, Ed. Jus, México, D.F., 1979.

C.E.G., *Tercer Encuentro Nacional Guadalupano, 5-7 diciembre de 1978*, Ed. Jus, México, D.F., 1979.

C.E.G., *Cuarto Encuentro Nacional Guadalupano, 4-6 diciembre de 1979*, Ed. Jus, México, D.F., 1980.

C. Salinas de la Mora, *Descubrimiento de un busto humano en los ojos de la Virgen de Guadalupe*, Ed. Tradición, México, D.F., 1980.

S. González Medina, *El acontecimiento del Tepeyac, mensaje de Salvación*, Ed. San José del Altillo, México, D.F., 1981.

C. Siller, *Flor y canto del Tepeyac*, in *Servir* (numero speciale), Xalapa (Veracruz), 1981.

F. de la Maza, *El guadalupanismo mexicano*, Ed. Fondo de Cultura Económica, México, D.F., 1981.

P. Callahan - J.B. Smith, *La tilma de Juan Diego. ¿Tecnica o milagro?*, Ed. Alhambra Mexicana, México, D.F., 1981.

Aa.vv., *Congreso Mariológico, 450° Aniversario (1531-1981), Insigne y Nacional Basílica de Guadalupe*, Ed. Melo, México, D.F., 1983.

Aa.vv., *Conmemoración Guadalupana, Conmemoración Arquidiocesana, 450 años*, Imprenta Ideal, México, D.F., 1984.

M. Rángel Camacho, *Virtudes y fama de santidad de Juan Diego*, Ed. Jus, México, D.F., 1984.

J. Cervantes, *La evangelización guadalupana*, documento di *Señal*, 15 (1985), n. 23, pp. 17-22.

V. Maccagnan, *Guadalupe*, in *Nuovo Dizionario di Mariologia*, a cura di S. De Fiores e S. Meo, San Paolo, Cinisello Balsamo, 1985, pp. 655-669.

C. Perfetti, *Guadalupe. La "tilma" della Morenita*, San Paolo, Cinisello Balsamo, 1987; 1998 (*La Madonna di Guadalupe. Fascino e mistero d'una immagine*).

John Paul II, Lettera apostolica *Exaltavit humiles* del 6 maggio 1990: concessione del culto liturgico in onore del beato Juan Diego; originale latino in AAS 82 (1990), pp. 853-855.

A.M. Sada Lambretón, *Las Informaciones jurídicas de 1666 y el beato indio Juan Diego*, Hijas de María Inmaculada de Guadalupe, México, D.F., 1991.

E. O'Gorman, *Destierro de sombras*, U.N.A.M., México, D.F., 1991.

L. Guerrero, *Flor y canto del nacimiento de México*, Ed. Jus, México, D.F., 1992.

J. Romero Salinas, *Juan Diego: su peregrinación a los altares*, Ed. Paulinas, México, D.F., 1992.

L. Guerrero, *Los dos mundos de un indio santo. Cuestionario preliminar de la Beatificación de Juan Diego*, Ed. Cimiento, México, D.F., 1992.

X. Noguez, *Documentos guadalupanos. Un estudio sobre las fuentes de información tempranas en torno a las mariofanías del Tepeyac*, Ed. Fondo de Cultura Económica, México, D.F., 1993.

Aa.vv., *La Madre del Señor en la fe y la cultura de México. Actas del Simposio Mariológico de México, México, D.F., 4-6 de agosto de 1992*, Librería Parroquial de Clavería, México, D.F., 1993.

R. Nebel, *Santa María Tonantzin, Virgen de Guadalupe. Continuidad y transformación religiosa en México*, Ed. Fondo de Cultura Económica, México, D.F., 1995.

X. Escalada, SJ, *Enciclopedia Guadalupana*, Enciclopedia Guadalupana, A. C. Ed., México, D.F., 1995.

Foreign-language Studies
(relative to the historical context)

A. Caso, *El pueblo del sol*, Ed: Fondo de Cultura Económica, México, D.F., 1935.

Toribio de Benavente (known as Motolinía), *Historia de los Indios de Nueva España*, Ed. D. Sánchez, México, D.F., 1956 (new ed. 1984).

L. Lopetegui, SJ - F. Zubillaga, SJ, *Historia de la Iglesia en la América Española*, Biblioteca de Autores Cristianos, Madrid, 1965.

J. Soustelle, *La vida cotidiana de los aztecas en vísperas de la conquista*, Ed. Fondo de Cultura Económica, México, D.F., 1970.

B. Díaz del Castillo, *Historia verdadera de la conquista de la Nueva España*, Circulo de Lectores, Barcelona, 1971.

A.M. Garibay, *Historia de la literatura náhuatl*, Ed. Porrúa, México, D.F., 1971.

L. Sejourné, *Pensamiento y religión en el México antiguo*, Ed. Fondo de Cultura Económica, México, D.F., 1972.

M. León-Portilla, *La filosofía náhuatl*, U.N.A.M., México, D.F., 1974.

N. Davies, *Gli aztechi*, Editori Riuniti, Roma, 1975.

B. de Sahagún, *Historia general de las cosas de la Nueva España*, Porrúa, México, D.F., 1975.

F. de Aguilar, *Relación breve de la conquista de la Nueva España*, U.N.A.M., Instituto de Investigaciones Históricas, México, D.F., 1977.

J. Soustelle, *El universo de los aztecas*, Ed. Fondo de Cultura Económica, México, D.F., 1978.

M. León-Portilla, *Visión de los vencidos*, U.N.A.M., México, D.F., 1980.

M. Marcocchi, *Colonialismo, cristianesimo e culture extraeuropee*, Jaca Book, Milano, 1981.

G. de Mendieta, *Historia Eclesiástica Indiana*, Ed. México, México, D.F., 1984.

R. Ricard, *La conquista espiritual de México*, Ed. Fondo de Cultura Económica, México, D.F., 1986.

L.N. McAlister, *Dalla scoperta alla conquista. Spagna e Portogallo nel Nuovo Mondo (1492-1700)*, Il Mulino, Bologna, 1986.

P. Borges, *Misión y civilización de América*, Ed. Alhambra, Madrid, 1987.

X. Serrano, *Los primeros 50 años de evangelización en el mundo náhuatl*, Ed. La Cruz, México, D.F., 1991.

Pontificia Commissio pro America Latina, *Historia de la evangelización de América. Trayectoria, identidad y esperanza de un Continente. Actas Simposio Internacional, Ciudad del Vaticano, 11-14 de mayo de 1992*, Libreria Editrice Vaticana, Città del Vaticano, 1992.

Aa.vv., *L 'Europa e l'evangelizzazione del Nuovo Mondo*, a cura di L. Vaccaro, Centro Ambrosiano, Milano, 1995.

Glossary

Acátl ("C-1 Acátl"; the year of the god Quetzalcoátl; 1519 was such a
    year when the Spaniards arrived in Mexico)
amate (a tree whose bark, when treated, can be used as a kind of
    parchment)
amoxtli (Indian designs painted on sheets of *amate*)
audiencia (sp.; tribunal, court of justice; organ of government)
ayate (the *tilma* made from rough vegetable fibers taken from the
    maguey plant)
Aztecs (Mexicans who spoke Nahuatl)

barrio (sp.; quarter, a city district)

cacaxtli (poor person)
calmecác (high school)
calpul/lis (little elevations upon which were built a group of houses or a
    single large house)
calzada (sp.; main street)
cantar (sp.; song)
Chichimeca (northern Mexican tribe that migrated to the South)
coátl (serpent)
coyoltótotl (a bird)

ermita (sp.; hermitage, small chapel)

flor azteca (sp.; Aztec flower, a design in the form of a cross represent-
    ing the four cardinal points of the compass with the sun at the
    center; a symbol of Quetzalcoátl)

guerra florida (sp.; flower war, a sacred or ritual war of the Aztecs)

hacienda (sp.; a large estate or plantation)
huizache (thorn tree)

ichtli (fibers from the *maguey* used to make *ayate*)
in xochitl in cuicatl (flowers and song, beauty and poetry)

macehual/es (middle class made up of landowners and farmers)
maguey (Mexican agave plant, used for its fibers and the making of an
    alcoholic beverage)
Maya (population and language of Central America)

mecapal (a poor or wretched person)
mestizo, mestizaje (sp.; of mixed race)
Mexica (Mexican; the population derived from the intermarriage of the various pre-Columbian races)
mezquite (a thick stemmed shrub or small tree, similar to the acacia)
moreno (sp.; dark, brown)

Nahua, Nahuatl (an ethnic-linguistic group in Mexico)
nemonteni (5 special days during the Aztec calendar year when extraordinary events were expected to take place; it was precisely during these days that the Spaniards arrived in Mexico)
noche triste (sp.; "the Night of Sorrow," June 30 - July 1, 1520)
nopal (Indian fig tree)

pochteca (the merchant class)
provisor (sp.; ecclesiastical judge)

quetzal (a bird; symbol of the sky and rain)

repartimiento (sp.; repartition or redistribution of the Indians)

tecuhtli (the ruling class made up of the nobles)
telpochcalli (public schools)
tilma (Indian mantle made from fibers taken from the *maguey* plant)
tira (sp.; a printing on paper, leather, or cloth)
tlacotl/e (lower class made up of slaves)
tlacuilo (expert in pictographs)
tlamaitl (the social class made up of field hands and manual laborers)
tlamatinime (wise, applied to both persons and books)
tlatoani ("he who speaks," that is, the king)
tlatocán (the supreme council in charge of governing the city)
Toltecs (the Mexican population whose native tongue was Nahuatl)
tonacatlapan ("the place from which we have all come")
Tóxcal (the month corresponding to May)
tzinitzcán (a bird)

viruela (purple)

xochitlalpan ("place where flowers abound")

Index

137

ST PAULS

This book was designed and published by St. Pauls/ Alba House, the publishing arm of the Society of St. Paul, an international religious congregation of priests and brothers dedicated to serving the Church through the communications media. For information regarding this and associated ministries of the Pauline Family of Congregations, write to the Vocation Director, Society of St. Paul, 7050 Pinehurst, Dearborn, Michigan 48126. Phone (313) 582-3798 or check our internet site, www.albahouse.org